THE STARTUP CODEBOOK

From Developer to Entrepreneur

Anish Bilas Panta

Table of Contents

ISBN-13: 9789937-1-4467

Anish Bilas Panta

Email: books@miocache.com

Website: books.miocache.com

First Edition: 2023

Disclaimer: The information provided in this book is based on factual content and the author's experiences. The author and publisher are not liable for any actions taken based on the contents of this book. Readers are advised to seek professional advice and conduct their research before making any business or financial decisions.

The Startup CodeBook

Introduction

Welcome to the enthralling world of "The Startup Codebook: From Developer to Entrepreneur." Within the pages of this compelling non-fiction guide, we embark on an enlightening journey that seamlessly bridges the gap between coding prowess and entrepreneurial brilliance. Whether you're a seasoned developer eager to ascend to new heights or an aspiring entrepreneur yearning to turn tech dreams into tangible success, this book is a treasure trove of knowledge that will steer you through the exhilarating and challenging landscape of startups.

In the opening chapters, we unlock the secrets behind why developers make exceptional startup founders. Their innate problem-solving abilities, technical expertise, and profound understanding of technology empower them to lead and drive entrepreneurial endeavors with unparalleled proficiency. As we delve into key considerations for developer-led startups, we equip you with the necessary insights to navigate the thrilling world of entrepreneurship with confidence and foresight.

Ideation and Validation form the heartbeat of successful startups, and we illuminate the path to discovering and validating groundbreaking ideas. Embracing lean methodologies and rapid prototyping, developers can efficiently breathe life into their concepts and test them in the dynamic marketplace, ensuring they gain the competitive edge they deserve.

With our compass set on "The Startup Landscape," we immerse ourselves in the vibrant startup ecosystem, uncovering the latest trends and illuminating the diverse funding models available to developer-founders. Understanding the intricacies of the landscape is vital for charting a course towards sustainable growth and prosperity.

Carefully selecting the right tech stack serves as the building blocks of a thriving startup. In "Choosing the Right Tech Stack," we guide you through the art of evaluating technologies and frameworks, enabling you to make informed decisions that foster scalability, performance, and development efficiency.

Moving forward, we fortify the foundation with insights on building the tech infrastructure. Unleashing the power of software architecture and design principles, we lay the groundwork for seamless scalability, superior performance, and uncompromising security, safeguarding user data and trust.

With the foundation solidified, we embark on the thrilling journey of "Developing a Minimum Viable Product (MVP)." By embracing agile methodologies and iterative development, we demonstrate how developers can create an MVP roadmap, prioritize features, and glean essential feedback for continuous refinement.

In a rapidly evolving technological landscape, "Leveraging Cloud Technologies" takes center stage. Cloud computing's boundless benefits empower startups to harness scalable infrastructure and platform services, delivering a seamless user experience while optimizing costs.

Venturing into the dynamic realm of funding and investment strategies, we uncover the allure of bootstrapping and the allure of external investors. As we traverse the fundraising landscape, you'll be well-equipped to approach investors as a developer-founder, ensuring your venture secures the support it deserves.

The crescendo of our journey is marked by the grand "Product Launch and Growth Strategies." We uncover the art of launching your product to the market and unleashing growth-hacking techniques for developers. Armed with the knowledge of data analytics, your product will be primed for continuous optimization and sustained growth.

In the age of innovation, we explore the exciting possibilities in "Incorporating Artificial Intelligence (AI)." As we unravel AI's myriad applications for startups, you'll gain insights on integrating machine learning and data-driven insights to elevate your startup's offerings to unparalleled heights.

"Building a Strong Team" is the cornerstone of startup success. Our guidance on hiring, managing developers, and fostering a culture of innovation and collaboration will ensure you construct a cohesive and formidable team, poised for excellence.

Technical challenges may loom on the horizon, but we equip you with the tools to overcome them in "Overcoming Technical Hurdles." As we tackle common obstacles and offer techniques for scaling infrastructure and managing technical debt, your code quality will stand the test of time.

With your startup poised for success, "Marketing and Branding for Developers" takes center stage. Crafting a compelling brand identity and developer-focused marketing strategies, we empower you to build a loyal community and tap into the vast potential of developer networks.

As we draw towards our inspiring conclusion, "Lessons from Successful Startup Founders" invites you to partake in insightful interviews and captivating case studies of developer-founders. Learn from their triumphs, setbacks, and invaluable wisdom, as they share key insights and advice for aspiring developer-founders.

With each turn of the page, "The Startup Codebook: From Developer to Entrepreneur" beckons you to embrace entrepreneurship and transform your vision into an awe-inspiring reality. The world of startups awaits your boundless potential, and this comprehensive guide is your steadfast companion on this thrilling odyssey of innovation, resilience, and triumph. So, buckle up and embark on the journey of a lifetime!

Chapter 1
Embracing Entrepreneurship

Why developers make great startup founders

Welcome to the exhilarating world of startup development! As a developer with extensive experience, you possess a unique combination of skills and qualities that make you well-suited for success in the startup landscape. Your technical expertise, honed through years of coding and problem-solving, empowers you to transform ideas into tangible products. With a deep understanding of technology, you can navigate the complexities of software development, select the most suitable tech stack, and optimize resources efficiently. Moreover, your entrepreneurial mindset, coupled with your ability to adapt to rapidly evolving technologies, enables you to seize opportunities, overcome challenges, and drive innovation. Embark on this incredible entrepreneurial journey and unleash the full potential of your technical prowess.

The Power of Technical Expertise

Developers bring a wealth of technical expertise to the table, making them invaluable assets in the startup realm. Their deep understanding of software development, programming languages, and problem-solving methodologies empowers them to transform ideas into functional software solutions. This ability to write code and build products from scratch gives them a significant advantage in creating a minimum viable product (MVP) to test and validate their startup concept.

Drawing from the experiences of several developer-turned-founders, it becomes evident how their coding skills enabled them to develop innovative products that solved pressing problems in the market. By leveraging their technical knowledge, they were able to iterate quickly, gather user feedback, and refine their products based on real-life usage scenarios.

Having a solid foundation in software development allows founders to make informed decisions about technology stack selection, system architecture, and scalability. They understand the intricacies of different programming languages and frameworks, enabling them to choose the most suitable tools for their startup's needs. This technical acumen gives them the ability to build robust and scalable software solutions that can adapt to changing market demands.

Furthermore, the technical expertise of developer-founders allows for effective communication with the development team. They can articulate their vision and requirements clearly, bridging the gap between business goals and technical implementation. This alignment is critical for ensuring that the product development process is efficient and effective.

As a developer-turned-founder, your deep understanding of software development, problem-solving methodologies, and emerging technologies gives you a distinct advantage in the startup landscape. Embrace your technical prowess, leverage your coding skills, and embark on an incredible entrepreneurial journey where you can turn your innovative ideas into reality.

The Developer's Problem-Solving Mindset

One of the defining traits of developers is their exceptional problem-solving mindset. Developers excel at breaking down complex problems into smaller, manageable components, employing analytical thinking, and devising innovative solutions. This ability to think critically and approach challenges with a systematic mindset is invaluable when navigating the unpredictable terrain of startups.

Throughout your career as a developer, you have honed your problem-solving skills, troubleshooting code, and finding efficient solutions. These skills can be transferred to various aspects of startup development, such as product design, user experience, and quality assurance. Embracing this problem-solving mindset will help you identify potential obstacles, anticipate challenges, and pivot swiftly when necessary.

In the startup landscape, you will encounter a myriad of challenges. From limited resources and tight deadlines to market competition and evolving customer needs, startups are a breeding ground for problems. However, as a developer-founder, you possess the unique ability to approach these challenges with a calm and calculated approach. Your experience in debugging code and finding elegant solutions translates well into problem-solving for your startup. You can analyze the root causes of issues, consider different approaches, and implement creative solutions to overcome obstacles.

Moreover, your problem-solving mindset extends beyond technical challenges. As a founder, you will face strategic decisions, operational hurdles, and market uncertainties. Your ability to break down complex problems into manageable components and consider multiple perspectives will enable you to make informed choices. You will be able to assess risks, evaluate trade-offs, and devise strategies that align with your startup's goals.

The problem-solving mindset of developers also fosters a culture of continuous improvement within startups. You understand the importance of learning from mistakes, gathering feedback, and iterating on your products and processes. This iterative approach allows you to adapt to market demands, incorporate user feedback, and deliver high-quality solutions. By continuously refining your startup's offerings and operations, you increase your chances of success in the competitive startup landscape.

Embrace your problem-solving skills, apply them to all aspects of your startup development, and navigate the entrepreneurial journey with confidence.

Continuous Learning and Adaptability

The field of software development is constantly evolving, requiring developers to be lifelong learners. Your ability to adapt to new technologies, programming frameworks, and industry trends is a significant advantage in the fast-paced startup ecosystem. Embracing continuous learning ensures that you stay up to date with the latest advancements and remain at the forefront of innovation.

As a seasoned developer, you understand the importance of keeping your skills sharp and embracing new tools and methodologies. This agility and thirst for knowledge will empower you to adapt to changing market dynamics, seize emerging opportunities, and build products that stay relevant in a rapidly evolving tech landscape.

In the startup world, being adaptable is crucial for success. Startups operate in a dynamic environment where market conditions, customer preferences, and competitive landscapes can shift rapidly. Your ability to learn and adapt quickly allows you to respond to these changes effectively. You can identify emerging trends, understand their implications for your startup, and adjust your strategies accordingly. This adaptability enables you to pivot your product, target new markets, or explore innovative business models to stay ahead of the competition.

Continuous learning also fosters a culture of innovation within your startup. By staying updated on the latest technologies and industry trends, you can identify new opportunities and leverage them to create unique value propositions. Your knowledge of cutting-edge tools and methodologies allows you to experiment, iterate, and develop innovative solutions that differentiate your startup from others in the market.

Furthermore, your commitment to continuous learning and adaptability sets an example for your team. By prioritizing learning and embracing change, you create a culture of growth and innovation within your startup. This encourages your team members to develop their skills, explore new ideas, and contribute to the overall success of the company.

Embrace the opportunity to learn and grow, stay abreast of the latest industry trends, and apply your knowledge to adapt your startup's strategies and products. By remaining agile and open to change, you position yourself for long-term success in the ever-evolving startup ecosystem.

Resourcefulness and Efficiency

Developers often operate in resource-constrained environments, encouraging resourcefulness and efficient problem-solving. These traits are invaluable in the early stages of a startup when budgets are tight, and you need to make the most of limited resources. Your ability to find creative solutions, optimize processes, and make efficient use of available tools and technologies will give your startup a competitive edge.

Throughout your career, you have likely encountered situations where you needed to accomplish tasks with limited resources or tight deadlines. These experiences have fostered a mindset of efficiency and a keen eye for optimizing processes. Embracing this resourcefulness will enable you to make the most of your startup's resources, maximizing productivity and minimizing waste.

As a developer-turned-founder, you possess the skills to identify areas where automation, streamlining, or outsourcing can enhance efficiency. You understand the value of leveraging existing tools and technologies to accelerate development cycles and reduce costs. This resourceful approach allows you to achieve more with less, stretching your startup's resources and increasing its chances of success.

Furthermore, your knack for problem-solving and optimization extends beyond technical aspects. You can apply these skills to various facets of your startup, such as operations, marketing, and customer acquisition. By identifying bottlenecks, eliminating inefficiencies, and making strategic decisions, you can create a lean and agile organization.

Embrace your ability to find creative solutions, optimize processes, and make efficient use of available resources. By leveraging your expertise and applying a resourceful mindset, you can drive your startup towards success, even in challenging and resource-constrained environments.

Key Considerations for Developer-Led Startups

Launching a startup as a developer offers unique advantages, but it's essential to approach it with careful consideration. In this section, we delve into the key factors that will guide you through the startup landscape and establish a solid foundation for your entrepreneurial journey. From understanding market dynamics to embracing agile methodologies, we explore how to leverage your technical expertise effectively. We'll also discuss the importance of building a diverse and complementary team, managing resources efficiently, and staying adaptable in the face of challenges. By addressing these considerations head-on, you'll be better equipped to navigate the exciting yet demanding path of a developer-led startup.

The Developer's Balancing Act: Technical Mastery and Business Savvy

Launching a successful startup as a developer requires a delicate balance between technical expertise and essential business skills. As a developer, you have mastered the art of coding and possess a deep understanding of technology. However, to navigate the challenges of entrepreneurship, it's crucial to expand your knowledge beyond code. Acquiring business skills such as market research, customer validation, marketing strategies, financial management, and effective communication will empower you to make informed decisions and engage with stakeholders.

While the idea of venturing into unfamiliar business domains may seem daunting, rest assured that it's a journey many successful developer-founders have embarked upon. By seeking out resources, attending workshops, and collaborating with mentors, you can develop your business acumen over time. Striking a balance between technical expertise and business knowledge is key to navigating the complexities of running a startup effectively.

Expanding your skill set to include business acumen will enable you to speak the language of investors, devise effective strategies, and make decisions that resonate with your target market and customers. Embracing this holistic approach positions you for long-term success and empowers you to confidently lead your developer-led startup into the ever-evolving world of entrepreneurship.

Building a Complementary Team

In addition to your technical skills, assembling a complementary team is vital for the success of your startup. As you embark on your entrepreneurial journey, it's essential to surround yourself with individuals who bring diverse expertise to the table. Collaborating with co-founders or team members who possess skills in areas like marketing, sales, operations, or finance will greatly enhance your startup's chances of success.

Let's consider the story of Jane, a software developer who transitioned into a founder role. Jane identified a gap in the market for a productivity app and utilized her technical expertise to develop a user-friendly solution. However, she quickly realized that to truly flourish, she needed to build a team that complemented her strengths. With this in mind, she sought out a co-founder who had a solid background in marketing and user acquisition.

By joining forces with a co-founder who brought expertise in these areas, Jane formed a dynamic team that combined technical excellence with business savvy. This partnership allowed them to not only develop a top-notch product but also effectively market and acquire users for their startup. The collaborative approach and diverse perspectives within the team propelled their startup to great heights.

By building a complementary team, you'll have access to a diverse skill set that covers all critical aspects of running a startup. This enables you to tackle challenges from multiple angles, leverage each team member's strengths, and foster an environment of innovation and growth. Remember, success in the startup world is rarely achieved alone; it's the collective effort and expertise of a well-rounded team that drives extraordinary results.

Embracing the Entrepreneurial Mindset

Transitioning from a developer to a startup founder requires a shift in mindset. Embracing an entrepreneurial mindset is crucial for navigating the challenges and uncertainties that come with startup development. It involves taking calculated risks, embracing failure as a learning opportunity, and being open to stepping outside your comfort zone.

Consider the example of Alex, a software developer who embarked on a startup journey. Initially, Alex was focused solely on coding and technical aspects. However, as the startup progressed, Alex realized the importance of adopting an entrepreneurial mindset. This shift allowed Alex to think more strategically, identify business opportunities, and adapt to market demands.

Embracing an entrepreneurial mindset empowers you to view setbacks as opportunities for growth and learning. It encourages you to think innovatively, take decisive action, and persevere in the face of challenges. By cultivating this mindset, you'll develop the resilience and determination needed to overcome obstacles and drive your startup forward.

Remember, as a developer-led startup founder, you possess a unique combination of technical expertise and entrepreneurial drive. Embracing the entrepreneurial mindset will unlock your full potential and enable you to navigate the complex and dynamic world of startups with confidence. Embrace the mindset of an entrepreneur, and watch as your startup transforms from an idea into a thriving reality.

The Story of Sarah

In Sarah's journey, she faced numerous obstacles and setbacks. There were times when she doubted herself and encountered unforeseen challenges. However, her entrepreneurial mindset kept her focused and resilient. She viewed failures as valuable learning experiences and used them to iterate and improve her platform.

Sarah's entrepreneurial mindset also played a crucial role in her ability to adapt to market changes and customer feedback. She actively sought feedback from designers and clients using her platform, incorporating their insights into future updates and feature enhancements. This iterative approach allowed her to continuously optimize the user experience and stay ahead of the competition.

Through her determination and entrepreneurial spirit, Sarah successfully grew her startup into a leading platform in the freelance design industry. Today, her platform connects thousands of designers with clients worldwide, providing a seamless and efficient way to collaborate on creative projects.

Sarah's story serves as an inspiration for developer-led startups. It showcases the importance of embracing an entrepreneurial mindset, acquiring business knowledge, and continuously learning and adapting in the ever-changing startup landscape. By combining technical expertise with an entrepreneurial mindset, developers like Sarah can pave the way for innovative and successful startups.

As you embark on your own startup journey, remember Sarah's story and the lessons it holds. Embrace the entrepreneurial mindset, seek opportunities to expand your skill set, and stay resilient in the face of challenges. With the right mindset and a passion for innovation, you too can build a thriving startup that leaves a lasting impact on the world.

****

As a developer-turned-startup-founder, you have a unique advantage in the entrepreneurial world. Your technical expertise, problem-solving skills, and passion for innovation position you for success. By embracing the key considerations discussed in this chapter and nurturing your entrepreneurial mindset, you are well-equipped to navigate the challenges and seize the opportunities that lie ahead.

Remember, your journey as a developer-turned-founder is filled with immense potential. Embrace the opportunities, learn from experiences, and leverage your technical expertise to build a startup that makes a lasting impact in the entrepreneurial world.

Chapter 2
From Inspiration to Reality: Ideation and Validation

Transforming an idea into a thriving startup necessitates a robust groundwork founded on inventive ideation, thorough market research, and effective validation. To begin, the process of generating startup ideas involves fostering a culture of creativity and encouraging innovative thinking. We will explore brainstorming techniques, problem-solving frameworks, and the art of identifying unmet needs within the market. By honing these skills, you will be able to conceive unique and viable startup ideas.

Once you have a collection of ideas, the next step is to validate their feasibility and potential for success. This entails conducting thorough market research to understand the competitive landscape, target audience, and market trends. By leveraging various research methods such as surveys, interviews, and data analysis, you can gain valuable insights into the market demand for your idea.

Furthermore, lean methodologies and rapid prototyping play a crucial role in the startup journey. Adopting a lean approach allows you to iterate quickly, test hypotheses, and gather feedback from potential customers. By building minimum viable products (MVPs) or prototypes, you can validate your assumptions, identify shortcomings, and refine your ideas before investing significant resources.

In parallel with these steps, it is essential to identify a specific target market for your startup idea. Understanding your potential customers' needs, preferences, and pain points enables you to tailor your product or service to meet their demands effectively. Additionally, assessing market fit ensures that your idea aligns with the market dynamics and has a competitive advantage.

Unleashing Creativity: Techniques for Generating Startup Ideas

The journey of building a startup starts with a spark of inspiration. To generate compelling startup ideas, it's essential to unleash your creativity and explore various avenues. Here are a few techniques that can help stimulate your idea generation process:

Problem Identification

Identifying problems or pain points is a fundamental step in generating startup ideas. By recognizing challenges that exist in your own life or industries you are passionate about, you can uncover opportunities for innovative solutions. One effective approach is to observe and reflect on the difficulties you encounter on a daily basis. These may be inconveniences, inefficiencies, or gaps in existing products or services.

For instance, let's take the example of project management tools like Trello and Asana. The founders of these tools recognized the pain points faced by remote teams in managing tasks efficiently. They observed the need for a streamlined and collaborative solution that could enhance productivity and communication. This realization led to the development of user-friendly platforms that revolutionized project management for remote teams.

Similarly, when you identify pain points within an industry you are passionate about, you can uncover valuable opportunities for innovation. By understanding the challenges faced by individuals or businesses in that industry, you can envision solutions that address those pain points and provide substantial value.

It's important to note that problem identification is not limited to personal experiences or passions. Keeping abreast of industry trends, news, and emerging technologies can also unveil potential problems or gaps that can be addressed with innovative solutions. By staying curious and actively seeking out challenges, you can identify untapped opportunities and generate startup ideas that have the potential to make a significant impact.

Market Observation

Market observation is a crucial aspect of generating startup ideas. By paying attention to emerging trends, technological advancements, and gaps in the market, you can identify potential opportunities for innovation. To stay informed and aware, it is essential to actively engage in activities such as keeping up with industry news, attending conferences, and participating in online communities.

By staying updated on industry news, you can gain insights into the latest developments and trends shaping various sectors. This knowledge can serve as a foundation for identifying gaps or areas where existing solutions are lacking. Additionally, attending conferences and networking events provides opportunities to connect with professionals and experts in your field of interest, fostering valuable discussions and potential collaborations.

Engaging with online communities, such as forums, social media groups, or industry-specific platforms, allows you to interact with like-minded individuals and gain diverse perspectives. These communities can serve as a valuable source of information, enabling you to identify emerging needs or problems that are yet to be adequately addressed.

One notable example of market observation leading to successful startups is the rise of the sharing economy. As people began embracing the concept of sharing resources and services, platforms like Airbnb and Uber emerged to capitalize on this trend. These companies identified a gap in the market and leveraged technological advancements to create innovative solutions that disrupted traditional industries.

Customer-Centric Approach

Adopting a customer-centric approach is essential for generating startup ideas that meet the needs and desires of your target market. By putting yourself in the shoes of potential customers and empathizing with them, you can gain valuable insights. Conducting user interviews, surveys, and focus groups allows you to directly engage with your target audience and understand their pain points.

By actively listening to customers and gathering feedback, you can identify the challenges they face and the areas where existing solutions fall short. This information serves as a foundation for developing startup ideas that address these pain points and provide innovative solutions.

For example, Slack, a popular team communication tool, was born out of the founders' commitment to improving communication and collaboration in team environments. Through user research and empathizing with the frustrations experienced by teams, they were able to create a product that resonated with their target audience.

By taking a customer-centric approach, you can align your startup idea with the needs and desires of your potential customers. This not only increases the chances of success but also helps in building a strong and loyal customer base.

Remember, the key is to think outside the box, challenge assumptions, and explore untapped areas where innovation can thrive.

Lean Methodologies and Rapid Prototyping: Bringing Ideas to Life

Once you have a compelling startup idea, it's important to quickly validate its potential and minimize time and resource investment. Lean methodologies and rapid prototyping offer effective approaches for this purpose. The goal is to gather feedback early in the development process to iterate and refine your concept.

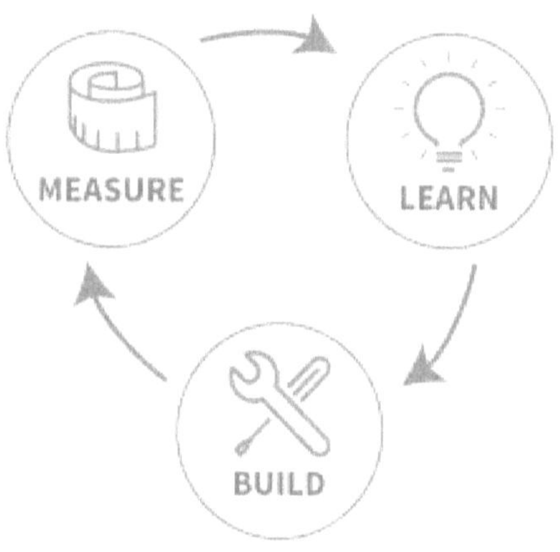

Build a Minimal Viable Product (MVP)

Building a Minimal Viable Product (MVP) is a crucial step in the startup journey. An MVP is a stripped-down version of your product that focuses on delivering the core value proposition to early adopters. By creating an MVP, you can validate your assumptions, test your solution in the market, and gather valuable feedback.

The concept of an MVP is to develop the most essential features and functionalities of your product or service, allowing you to launch quickly and start gaining insights from real users. This iterative approach helps you avoid spending excessive time and resources on building a fully-featured product before validating its viability.

Dropbox provides a notable example of an MVP success story. The initial version of Dropbox allowed users to store and share files in a simple folder structure. This basic functionality addressed a fundamental need for file synchronization and collaboration, and it resonated with early users. Dropbox was able to gather feedback, iterate, and enhance the product based on user input, leading to its eventual success.

By releasing an MVP, you can gather valuable insights into user behavior, preferences, and pain points. This feedback loop enables you to make informed decisions about the future direction of your product, iterate on features, and enhance the user experience.

Iterate Based on User Feedback

Once your MVP is in the hands of users, it is crucial to actively seek feedback and observe their interactions with your product. This user feedback serves as a valuable source of insights to drive the iterative process of improving your startup idea.

Actively listen to users and encourage them to provide feedback through surveys, interviews, or feedback forms. Analyze their behavior and observe how they navigate your product. This will help you identify pain points, areas of confusion, and opportunities for improvement.

By gathering user insights, you can make informed decisions about the next iterations of your product. Prioritize the feedback based on its impact and feasibility, and incorporate necessary changes to enhance user experience and address their needs.

A prominent example of a startup that evolved through continuous iterations based on user feedback is WhatsApp. Initially, the app was designed as a simple messaging platform, but the founders actively listened to user feedback and made iterative improvements over time. These improvements included features like voice messaging, file sharing, and end-to-end encryption. Through these iterations, WhatsApp transformed into a widely adopted messaging platform that addressed user needs and preferences.

Iterating based on user feedback ensures that your startup idea evolves to meet real user needs and preferences. It helps you stay agile, responsive, and customer-centric, ultimately increasing the chances of long-term success in the market.

Rapid Prototyping

Rapid prototyping is a valuable technique that can significantly aid in the development of your startup idea. By using prototyping tools and techniques, you can create interactive mockups or wireframes of your product, which serve as tangible representations of your vision.

Prototypes enable you to gather feedback from potential users, stakeholders, or investors at an early stage. By sharing these prototypes, you can solicit valuable insights and validate the usability, functionality, and overall concept of your product.

Prototyping tools such as InVision or Figma provide user-friendly interfaces and functionalities that allow you to simulate user interactions. These tools enable you to showcase the flow of your product, demonstrate specific features, and gather feedback on the user experience.

By creating rapid prototypes, you can iterate and refine your design and functionality based on feedback and user testing. This iterative process helps you uncover potential issues, make necessary improvements, and ensure that your final product meets user expectations and needs.

Rapid prototyping also offers cost and time benefits. By investing in prototypes before full-scale development, you can identify and address potential flaws or misunderstandings early on, saving resources and reducing the likelihood of costly rework.

Identifying a Target Market and Assessing Market Fit

To ensure startup success, it's crucial to identify a target market and evaluate market fit. This involves understanding the needs and preferences of your potential customers and aligning your idea accordingly.

Define Your Ideal Customer Profile

Defining your ideal customer profile is a crucial step in developing a successful startup. By identifying the characteristics of your target customers, such as demographics, behaviors, preferences, and pain points, you can tailor your product to meet their specific needs and effectively market it to the right audience.

Understanding your ideal customer profile enables you to align your product features, messaging, and marketing strategies with their expectations and preferences. By doing so, you increase the likelihood of attracting and retaining loyal customers.

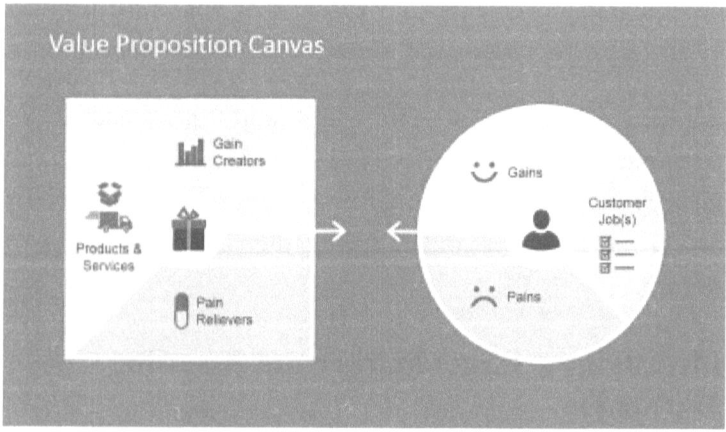

For example, suppose you are developing a fitness app. In that case, your target market might consist of health-conscious individuals who prefer convenient home workouts over traditional gym memberships. By defining this ideal customer profile, you can focus on creating features that cater to their specific needs, such as workout routines that can be easily performed at home, tracking tools for progress monitoring, or personalized recommendations based on their fitness goals.

Defining your ideal customer profile also helps in efficient resource allocation and targeting your marketing efforts. By understanding who your target customers are, you can allocate your resources towards channels and strategies that are most likely to reach and engage with them effectively.

Conduct Market Research

Market research play a pivotal role in shaping the success and viability of your venture. By analyzing the size of your target market, studying the competition, and understanding market trends, you can gain valuable insights that inform the viability and potential demand for your product or service.

Market research allows you to evaluate the size and growth potential of your target market. By understanding the number of potential customers and their purchasing power, you can assess the market's attractiveness and potential revenue opportunities. Additionally, analyzing market trends helps you stay informed about shifts in consumer behavior, emerging technologies, and industry dynamics, allowing you to adapt your offering accordingly.

Examining the competitive landscape is equally important. Identifying direct and indirect competitors, understanding their strengths and weaknesses, and studying their market positioning provides valuable insights. This analysis enables you to differentiate your product or service and identify unique selling points that can help you stand out in the market.

Market research also uncovers niche segments and untapped opportunities. By delving deep into specific market segments, you may discover underserved customer needs or gaps that your startup can address. For example, researching the e-commerce market might reveal a niche segment where your unique offering can thrive, providing a competitive advantage.

By conducting market research, you gather data-driven insights that help validate your startup idea, refine your target market, and make informed strategic decisions. It reduces the risk of entering a market blindly and increases the chances of delivering a product or service that resonates with customers.

Validate Market Fit

Engaging with potential customers, presenting your idea, and gathering feedback are key activities to assess market fit effectively.

To validate market fit, you can conduct surveys, run focus groups, or perform user tests. These methods enable you to directly engage with your target audience and gather their opinions, insights, and reactions. By listening to their feedback, you can identify if your solution effectively addresses their pain points and meets their needs.

Surveys provide a quantitative approach to collect data on customer preferences, while focus groups offer a more qualitative and interactive platform for in-depth discussions. User tests allow you to observe users interacting with your product or service, uncovering usability issues and gaining insights into user behavior.

The feedback and insights gathered through these validation methods are invaluable for refining your product or service and aligning it with the expectations of your target market. It helps you make informed decisions about product enhancements, positioning, and messaging.

By validating market fit, you can minimize the risk of developing a product that doesn't resonate with customers. It allows you to iterate and improve your offering based on real user feedback, increasing the chances of success in the market.

****

By thoroughly understanding your target market and ensuring market fit, you increase the chances of developing a product that resonates with customers and meets their needs.

Remember, successful startups are built on solid foundations of well-validated ideas, lean methodologies, and a deep understanding of the target market. By leveraging these techniques and approaches, you can enhance the likelihood of transforming your startup idea into a thriving reality. Stay curious, embrace feedback, and let your passion drive you towards entrepreneurial success.

Chapter 3
Navigating the Startup Landscape

In the dynamic and expansive realm of startups, it is essential to have a solid grasp of the landscape to position your venture for success. This chapter is dedicated to exploring the intricacies of the startup ecosystem, providing insights into current trends, various startup models, funding options, and strategies for navigating the competitive landscape and industry dynamics. By gaining a comprehensive understanding of the startup landscape, you can make informed decisions and seize opportunities that align with your entrepreneurial aspirations.

The startup landscape is constantly evolving, influenced by factors such as technological advancements, market trends, and consumer behavior. Staying abreast of these changes allows you to identify emerging opportunities and adapt your business strategy accordingly.

Additionally, understanding the different startup models, such as B2B (business-to-business), B2C (business-to-consumer), SaaS (software-as-a-service), or marketplace models, helps you determine the most suitable approach for your venture.

Moreover, funding options play a pivotal role in the startup journey. Exploring avenues such as bootstrapping, angel investors, venture capital, crowdfunding, or government grants can provide the necessary capital to fuel your growth.

Furthermore, navigating the competitive landscape requires careful analysis of competitors, market gaps, and differentiation strategies. Understanding industry dynamics and trends empowers you to make strategic decisions that position your startup for success.

By immersing yourself in the startup landscape, you gain insights that enable you to identify opportunities, mitigate risks, and optimize your entrepreneurial journey. This chapter equips you with the knowledge and tools to navigate the multifaceted startup ecosystem and leverage it to your advantage.

Exploring the Current Startup Ecosystem and Trends

The startup ecosystem is a vibrant and interconnected network comprising entrepreneurs, investors, support organizations, and technological advancements. It is constantly evolving, driven by innovation and market dynamics.

By exploring the startup landscape, you can gain valuable insights into the latest developments and shifts in industries and markets. This knowledge allows you to identify potential areas of growth and innovation, helping you stay ahead of the curve and capitalize on emerging opportunities.

Throughout this section, we will explore key components of the startup ecosystem, such as incubators and accelerators, startup communities, funding trends, and emerging technologies. By understanding these elements, you can navigate the startup landscape more effectively, make informed decisions, and position your venture for success.

Mapping the Startup Ecosystem

To navigate the startup landscape effectively, begin by mapping the key players, startup hubs, incubators, accelerators, and innovation centers in your region or on a global scale. Understanding the structure and dynamics of the ecosystem is crucial as it opens doors to valuable networking opportunities and access to essential resources. By exploring the vibrant communities and support networks within the startup ecosystem, you can find the guidance and nurturing needed to fuel your startup's growth.

Emerging Technologies

Remaining knowledgeable about the latest emerging technologies and their influence on the startup landscape is essential. Delve into the realms of artificial intelligence, blockchain, Internet of Things, augmented reality, and other transformative technologies that are shaping the startup ecosystem. By understanding these technologies, you can explore how they can be leveraged to create innovative solutions and gain a competitive edge in the market.

Artificial intelligence (AI) offers opportunities for automation, predictive analytics, and personalized user experiences. Blockchain technology provides decentralized and secure solutions for various industries, including finance and supply chain. The Internet of Things (IoT) enables interconnected devices and data-driven insights. Augmented reality (AR) enhances user experiences through interactive digital overlays.

By staying informed and embracing these emerging technologies, startups can disrupt industries, drive efficiency, and meet evolving customer demands. Understanding the potential applications and implications of these technologies empowers entrepreneurs to identify areas where they can make a significant impact and deliver value to customers.

Consider how AI can optimize processes or how blockchain can revolutionize data security and transparency. Explore how IoT can enable smart homes or how AR can enhance shopping experiences. By embracing these emerging technologies, startups can position themselves as pioneers, attract investment, and gain a competitive advantage in the ever-evolving startup landscape.

Industry-Specific Trends

Recognizing the distinct dynamics and trends within each industry is crucial for startup success. Explore industry-specific trends and disruptions that present opportunities for innovation and entrepreneurship. Stay updated on emerging markets, evolving customer needs, and regulatory changes that can significantly impact your startup's trajectory. By understanding the pulse of your industry, you can identify gaps and develop solutions that resonate with the market.

Every industry undergoes its unique transformations driven by technological advancements, changing consumer preferences, and market forces. By staying informed about the latest industry-specific trends, startups can anticipate shifts in demand, identify unmet needs, and tailor their offerings accordingly.

Monitor emerging markets to identify untapped opportunities that align with your startup's capabilities. As new regions or customer segments gain prominence, being at the forefront allows you to capture market share and establish a competitive edge.

Evolving customer needs and preferences are fundamental drivers of industry change. By closely following customer behavior, feedback, and market research, startups can align their products or services with the evolving demands of their target audience.

Furthermore, regulatory changes can significantly impact industry landscapes. Stay updated on relevant laws, policies, and compliance requirements to ensure your startup operates within legal boundaries and to identify areas where regulatory shifts can create new opportunities.

By actively monitoring and adapting to industry-specific trends, startups can position themselves as leaders, seize emerging opportunities, and create innovative solutions that address evolving market needs. Understanding the unique dynamics of your industry enables you to stay ahead of the competition, navigate challenges, and drive growth in a rapidly changing business environment.

Understanding Different Startup Models and Funding Options

Startups operate under various models, each with its own unique characteristics and considerations. Familiarizing yourself with different startup models and understanding funding options will help you make informed decisions about your own venture.

Bootstrapping: Nurturing Your Own Growth

The bootstrapping model is a strategic approach that many successful startups have embraced to fund their growth without external investors or loans. By relying on their own resources and revenue generation, entrepreneurs can maintain full control and flexibility over their business, shaping their vision and strategy according to their own values and long-term goals.

While bootstrapping offers control and autonomy, it comes with its share of challenges. Limited financial resources and slower growth compared to ventures backed by external funding are common hurdles. To succeed, bootstrapped startups like Dropbox and Basecamp had to be resourceful and creative in finding cost-effective solutions, fostering a culture of efficiency and resilience.

Bootstrapping is not a one-size-fits-all approach, and it may not be suitable for every startup. However, for those willing to embrace the challenges and maximize their available resources, bootstrapping can be a viable and empowering path to sustainable growth and success

Venture Capital: Partnering for Rapid Growth

Venture capital is a vital source of funding that fuels the growth and expansion of startups. Understanding the world of venture capital is essential for entrepreneurs seeking to scale their ventures rapidly. Venture capitalists invest in early-stage or high-potential startups in exchange for equity, providing the capital needed to accelerate growth and reach new milestones.

Exploring the realm of venture capital allows entrepreneurs to familiarize themselves with the funding process and expectations that come with it. Securing venture capital funding typically involves pitching your business to investors, showcasing your market opportunity, competitive advantage, and growth potential. It requires a compelling business plan, a solid team, and a clear path to profitability.

Venture capital brings more than just financial support. VCs often offer guidance, industry connections, and expertise to help startups navigate challenges and capitalize on opportunities. Partnering with the right venture capitalist can provide access to valuable resources, mentorship, and networks that can contribute to the startup's success.

However, it's important to note that venture capital may not be suitable for every startup. It typically comes with high growth expectations and dilution of ownership. Founders should carefully evaluate their business goals, growth trajectory, and long-term vision before pursuing venture capital funding.

Angel Investors: Guiding Your Early Steps

Angel investors play a crucial role in supporting startups during their early stages. Understanding the dynamics of angel investment is vital for entrepreneurs seeking funding and guidance. Angel investors are individuals who provide capital to startups in exchange for equity. They often bring not only financial support but also valuable expertise, networks, and mentorship.

One notable example of successful angel investment is the story of Airbnb. In the early days of Airbnb, founders Brian Chesky and Joe Gebbia struggled to secure funding from traditional investors. However, they found their first angel investor in Paul Graham, the co-founder of Y Combinator. Paul saw the potential in their unique concept of offering air mattresses in their apartment to travelers. He believed in the founding team's vision and provided them with a seed investment of $20,000.

Beyond the financial support, Paul Graham's mentorship and guidance proved invaluable for Airbnb's success. His experience and connections in the tech industry helped the founders refine their business model and connect with other influential investors and advisors. With Paul's support, Airbnb quickly gained traction and expanded into a global hospitality platform, revolutionizing the way people travel and find accommodations.

Discovering the investment criteria and preferences of angel investors is key to identifying potential partners. Angel investors typically focus on specific industries or sectors where they have domain expertise. They seek innovative ideas with high growth potential and a capable founding team. Researching and understanding the investment interests of angel investors helps entrepreneurs target the right individuals or groups for their startup.

Approaching potential angel investors requires a well-crafted pitch that highlights the value proposition, market opportunity, and growth potential of the startup. Demonstrating a clear vision, traction, and a solid plan for execution can attract the attention and interest of angel investors. Building a strong network and seeking introductions from trusted connections can also enhance the chances of connecting with angel investors.

Angel investors offer more than just financial support. Their experience and networks can provide invaluable guidance, mentorship, and industry connections. Entrepreneurs can leverage the expertise of angel investors to refine their business strategies, navigate challenges, and access additional funding sources.

Crowdfunding: Empowering the Community

Crowdfunding has emerged as a powerful tool for entrepreneurs to raise funds and engage a community of supporters. Understanding the concept of crowdfunding and its various models and platforms is crucial for those seeking alternative funding sources. Crowdfunding allows entrepreneurs to raise capital by collecting small contributions from a large number of individuals through online platforms.

One inspiring example of successful crowdfunding is the story of Pebble Technology, a startup that developed the Pebble smartwatch. In 2012, Pebble launched a crowdfunding campaign on Kickstarter, aiming to raise $100,000 to fund the production of their innovative smartwatch. To their surprise, the campaign went viral, and within a few weeks, they raised over $10 million, making it one of the most funded projects on Kickstarter at that time. The overwhelming support from the crowdfunding community not only provided Pebble with the necessary capital to bring their product to market but also generated significant media attention and consumer interest.

Exploring different crowdfunding models and platforms helps entrepreneurs identify the most suitable option for their startup. Some platforms operate on a donation-based model, where contributors receive non-financial rewards or simply support the cause. Others follow a reward-based model, where backers receive tangible rewards or pre-order products. Equity-based crowdfunding allows individuals to invest in a startup in exchange for equity shares, while debt-based crowdfunding involves borrowing money that needs to be repaid.

Crafting a compelling crowdfunding campaign is essential to attract and engage potential backers. It requires effectively communicating the value proposition, the impact of the startup, and the benefits of contributing. Creating engaging content, such as videos, images, and detailed project descriptions, helps captivate the audience and build trust. Leveraging social media and personal networks amplifies the reach and visibility of the crowdfunding campaign.

Crowdfunding goes beyond raising funds; it empowers entrepreneurs to build a community of supporters who believe in their vision. Engaging this community through regular updates, acknowledging contributions, and involving backers in the startup's journey fosters a sense of ownership and loyalty. The collective support and advocacy of the community can extend beyond the funding campaign and positively impact the startup's growth.

Navigating the Competitive Landscape and Industry Dynamics

To thrive in the competitive startup landscape, it is essential to navigate the industry dynamics effectively. By staying ahead of industry trends, identifying market opportunities, and leveraging your unique strengths, you can position your startup for success.

STRENGTHS

- What is your unique selling proposition?
- What are your competitive advantages?
- What resources do you have?
- What do customers like about your product?
- What do you do better than your competitors?
- What advantages do your staff members have?
- What assets does your company have?

WEAKNESSES

- Which areas of your business/projects could use improvement?
- What advantages does your company lack?
- What do your competitors do better than you?
- Which disadvantages do our workers/products have?
- Which internal factors interfere with your business success?

OPPORTUNITIES

- Does economic/political climate help you develop your business?
- Which external factors can give you an edge?
- How can market fluctuations aid you?
- Do these opportunities have temporary nature?

THREATS

- Who are your competitors?
- Which market areas are potentially dangerous for your business?
- Which trends can negatively affect your business?
- Is there a product/innovation on the market that will make your product/innovation outdated?

Competitor Analysis: Unveiling Your Advantages

Conducting a comprehensive competitor analysis is essential for understanding the competitive landscape and unveiling your advantages. By studying your direct and indirect competitors, you can identify their strengths, weaknesses, market positioning, and strategies. This analysis provides valuable insights into how you can differentiate your startup and highlight your unique value propositions.

To gather competitive intelligence, utilize various techniques such as researching public information, analyzing their marketing materials and online presence, and monitoring their customer feedback. By understanding your competitors' offerings, target market, pricing strategies, and customer satisfaction levels, you can identify areas where you can excel and stand out.

Leveraging the information gathered from competitor analysis, you can refine your product or service, optimize your marketing strategy, and enhance your value proposition. By focusing on your strengths and addressing the gaps left by your competitors, you can effectively position your startup in the market.

Remember that competitor analysis is an ongoing process, as the competitive landscape evolves. Continuously monitor and reassess your competitors to stay ahead of industry trends and adapt your strategies accordingly. By staying informed and leveraging competitive intelligence, you can maximize your advantages and drive the success of your startup.

Industry Trends and Disruptions: Seizing Opportunities

Staying informed about industry trends and disruptions is crucial for seizing opportunities. By keeping a pulse on market shifts, changing customer preferences, and emerging technologies, you can anticipate and capitalize on new avenues for growth.

Regularly research and analyze industry trends to identify potential opportunities or threats. Stay updated on market reports, industry publications, and thought leaders' insights to understand the direction in which your industry is heading. This knowledge enables you to adapt your strategies and position your startup accordingly.

Embracing emerging technologies can also be a game-changer for your startup. Explore how technologies such as artificial intelligence, blockchain, or virtual reality can be applied to your industry and create innovative solutions. By leveraging these technologies early on, you can gain a competitive advantage and attract early adopters.

Furthermore, be prepared to pivot your strategies when necessary. Disruptions can reshape industries overnight, and being agile and adaptable is key to surviving and thriving. Monitor the competitive landscape and customer feedback to identify signals for change and proactively adjust your business model, product offering, or market positioning.

By staying informed about industry trends and disruptions, you can position your startup to seize opportunities as they arise. Embrace innovation, adaptability, and a forward-thinking mindset to navigate the ever-changing startup landscape successfully.

Partnerships and Collaborations: Expanding Your Reach

Partnerships and collaborations can be powerful drivers of growth for startups. By exploring opportunities for collaboration within your industry, you can expand your reach and tap into new markets. Identify potential partners with complementary offerings or synergistic capabilities that can amplify the value you provide to customers.

Strategic alliances with established companies or organizations can bring numerous benefits, such as access to their customer base, distribution channels, expertise, or resources. Look for mutually beneficial partnerships that align with your business goals and values. Collaborating with industry leaders or complementary startups can help you gain credibility and accelerate your growth.

When pursuing partnerships, it is crucial to foster open communication, trust, and shared objectives. Clearly define roles, responsibilities, and expectations to ensure a successful collaboration. Regularly assess the progress and impact of the partnership to ensure it continues to align with your strategic objectives.

Partnerships and collaborations can open doors to new possibilities and provide a competitive edge in the market. By expanding your reach through strategic alliances, you can leverage the strengths of your partners, access new markets, and enhance the value proposition for your customers. Embrace the power of collaboration to fuel the growth and success of your startup.

****

To navigate the startup landscape successfully, it is crucial to have a comprehensive understanding of the ecosystem, funding options, and competitive dynamics. By staying informed about emerging trends, exploring funding sources, and analyzing the competitive landscape, you can position your startup for success. Remain agile, adapt to changing circumstances, and seize opportunities that align with your vision.

Chapter 4
Choosing the Right Tech Stack

Choosing the right tech stack is a critical decision that can significantly impact the success of your venture. The tech stack serves as the foundation of your product, determining its scalability, performance, and development efficiency. Striking the right balance between technical capabilities and business needs is essential to ensure the smooth operation and growth of your startup. By making informed decisions and selecting a robust tech stack, you can lay a solid foundation for your product's success in the competitive market.

Evaluating Different Technologies and Frameworks

Understanding the Technology Landscape

In the ever-changing world of technology, it is crucial for startups to stay informed about the latest advancements and trends. By exploring different technologies, you can understand their specific features, strengths, weaknesses, and areas of application. This knowledge will help you make informed decisions when selecting the components of your tech stack.

Furthermore, staying abreast of current industry trends is vital for anticipating the future direction of technology. By identifying emerging technologies, such as artificial intelligence, blockchain, Internet of Things, or machine learning, you can assess their potential impact on your startup and evaluate whether incorporating them into your tech stack can provide a competitive advantage.

Understanding the technology landscape not only allows you to make informed decisions about the tools and platforms you use but also enables you to engage in meaningful discussions with your development team and technical partners. It fosters a shared understanding of the technological possibilities and sets the stage for effective collaboration in building innovative solutions.

By continuously exploring the technology landscape and being proactive in adapting to new developments, you can position your startup to leverage the power of cutting-edge technologies and stay ahead of the competition.

Assessing Compatibility and Integration

Ensuring compatibility and seamless integration among the components of your tech stack is essential. Consider the ease of integrating your chosen technologies with external systems, third-party APIs, and services that are crucial to your startup's success. Evaluate the level of support and documentation available for integration, as well as the potential challenges and dependencies that may arise.

Smooth collaboration between the various components of your tech stack is also paramount. Explore strategies to ensure effective communication and coordination between different technologies, such as using well-defined interfaces, following industry standards, and adopting best practices for system architecture.

By carefully assessing compatibility and integration, you can avoid potential roadblocks and technical bottlenecks in the development process. This allows for a seamless flow of data and functionality across your stack, leading to improved performance, scalability, and overall user experience.

Furthermore, considering compatibility and integration during the tech stack selection process enables you to future-proof your startup. By choosing technologies that can easily adapt and integrate with evolving systems and technologies, you can ensure that your product remains flexible and adaptable to future needs and market demands.

By prioritizing compatibility and integration, you lay a solid foundation for a cohesive and efficient tech stack that can effectively support the growth and success of your startup.

Evaluating Performance and Scalability

Understanding the performance characteristics of different technologies and frameworks is essential. Explore benchmarks and performance metrics to assess how well a technology or framework can handle high traffic, data processing, and other performance-intensive tasks. Consider factors such as response time, throughput, and resource utilization to make informed decisions about the components of your tech stack.

Scalability is another critical aspect to consider. Evaluate how well the technologies and frameworks in your stack can scale as your user base and data volume grow. Assess their ability to handle increased load and concurrent users. Explore optimization techniques, such as caching, horizontal scaling, or distributed computing, to ensure your startup can meet the demands of increased user demand and business growth.

By carefully evaluating performance and scalability, you can build a robust tech stack that can handle the challenges of a growing user base and provide a seamless experience to your customers. It allows your startup to be agile, responsive, and capable of scaling its infrastructure as needed to accommodate future growth.

Additionally, optimizing performance and scalability from the early stages of development helps in minimizing technical debt and costly rearchitecting efforts down the line. It allows your startup to be well-prepared for future scalability challenges and ensures a smooth user experience even during peak demand.

Community Support and Documentation

When choosing a tech stack for your startup, the strength of the community surrounding the technologies and the availability of comprehensive documentation are crucial factors to consider. A vibrant developer community can provide valuable support, insights, and resources. Explore online forums, discussion boards, and social media groups to gauge the level of engagement and knowledge sharing within the community. A strong community can offer assistance, guidance, and innovative ideas that can benefit your development process.

Comprehensive documentation plays a vital role in accelerating development and troubleshooting. Assess the availability and quality of documentation for the technologies and frameworks you're considering. Look for well-documented APIs, libraries, and frameworks that provide clear explanations, tutorials, and examples. Robust documentation enables your development team to understand and utilize the features and functionalities of the technologies effectively.

Additionally, documentation helps your team stay up to date with best practices, version updates, and security considerations. It serves as a valuable resource for onboarding new team members and facilitating knowledge transfer within your startup. This fosters a collaborative environment and empowers your team to navigate challenges, stay updated with the latest advancements, and make informed decisions throughout the development process.

Factors to Consider When Selecting a Tech Stack

Business Requirements and Product Vision

To build a solid tech stack for your startup, it is crucial to align it with your business requirements and product vision. Start by clearly defining your business requirements and understanding your product vision. Consider factors such as your target market, scalability requirements, security needs, regulatory compliance, and industry standards. Identify the core functionalities and features that your product must have to meet the needs of your customers.

Next, evaluate how different technologies and frameworks align with your business requirements and product vision. Assess their capabilities, flexibility, and suitability for your startup's goals. Consider factors like the learning curve for your development team, the availability of relevant libraries and tools, and the long-term support and maintenance requirements.

Ensure that your chosen tech stack can scale alongside your business as it grows. Anticipate future needs and evaluate the scalability of the technologies you are considering. Choose technologies that can accommodate increased user demand, handle larger datasets, and support future feature enhancements.

Development Team Skills and Expertise

The expertise and skills of your development team are key factors to consider when selecting a tech stack. Assess the proficiency of your team members and their familiarity with different technologies and frameworks. Consider their strengths, preferences, and ability to adapt and learn new technologies.

Evaluate the existing skills within your team and identify technologies that align with their expertise. Leverage their knowledge and experience to make informed decisions about the tech stack. This approach can help you leverage their strengths and increase development efficiency.

At the same time, be open to exploring new technologies that can empower your team to excel. Consider the learning curve associated with adopting new technologies and evaluate the resources and support available to help your team acquire the necessary skills.

Fostering a learning culture within your development team is also crucial. Encourage continuous learning and provide opportunities for skill development, such as training programs or workshops. This will enable your team to adapt to new technologies and stay up to date with industry trends.

Striking a balance between leveraging existing skills and exploring new technologies can help you build a tech stack that maximizes your team's potential and drives the success of your startup.

Time-to-Market and Development Efficiency

For startups, getting your product to market quickly is often a critical factor for success. When selecting a tech stack, consider how different technologies and frameworks can expedite your development process.

Evaluate the availability of libraries, tools, and frameworks that facilitate rapid prototyping, code reuse, and development efficiency. Look for technologies that offer robust documentation and a supportive community, as these resources can significantly accelerate your development timeline.

Embrace agile methodologies and iterative development practices to streamline your time-to-market journey. Break down your product development into smaller, manageable tasks and prioritize features based on their impact and feasibility. This approach allows you to release minimum viable products and gather user feedback early on, enabling you to iterate and improve your product while it's in the market.

Additionally, consider the scalability and maintainability of the technologies and frameworks you choose. Scalable solutions allow you to handle increased user demand as your startup grows, while maintainable code ensures easier bug fixes and future updates.

By carefully considering time-to-market and development efficiency, you can select a tech stack that empowers your team to build and launch your product quickly and efficiently.

Cost Considerations

Financial considerations are crucial for startups operating on limited budgets. When selecting a tech stack, it's important to evaluate the cost implications associated with your choices.

Assess the licensing fees, if any, associated with the technologies and frameworks you're considering. Consider the hosting costs and infrastructure requirements, such as cloud services or dedicated servers. Evaluate the availability of affordable resources and talent within your chosen stack, as hiring developers with specialized skills can impact your budget.

Strive for a balance between cost-effectiveness and long-term scalability. While it may be tempting to opt for the cheapest options, it's important to ensure that your chosen tech stack can support your startup's growth and handle increased user demand without incurring significant additional costs.

Consider open-source technologies and frameworks that offer cost savings without compromising on functionality and reliability. Leverage the expertise of your development team to identify cost-effective solutions and optimize resource utilization.

By carefully evaluating the cost considerations associated with your tech stack, you can make informed decisions that align with your startup's financial capabilities while still meeting your technical requirements.

Balancing Scalability, Performance, and Development Efficiency

Scalability Considerations

Scalability is a critical factor for startups aiming for growth and success. When evaluating your tech stack, it's important to consider scalability and ensure that your chosen technologies and architectural patterns can support the increasing demands of your application.

Explore different scaling strategies such as horizontal and vertical scaling. Horizontal scaling involves adding more machines or servers to distribute the workload, while vertical scaling involves upgrading the existing infrastructure to handle increased traffic and data processing.

Consider distributed systems that allow you to break down your application into smaller, interconnected components, enabling better scalability and fault tolerance. Explore caching mechanisms to reduce the load on your backend systems and improve response times. Load balancing techniques can also help distribute the incoming traffic evenly across multiple servers or instances.

Designing your application with scalability in mind is crucial. Consider decoupling components, implementing asynchronous processing, and leveraging technologies that support auto-scaling and dynamic resource allocation.

By considering scalability in your tech stack selection and architectural design, you can ensure that your startup can handle increasing user demands and growth without compromising performance or user experience.

Performance Optimization Techniques

Optimizing the performance of your application is crucial for delivering a smooth user experience and maintaining high levels of user satisfaction. Within your chosen tech stack, there are various techniques you can employ to improve performance and optimize resource usage.

One effective approach is to implement caching mechanisms. Caching can reduce the load on your backend systems by storing frequently accessed data or computed results in memory. This helps to improve response times and reduce latency, resulting in a faster and more responsive application.

Additionally, optimizing your database can have a significant impact on performance. Techniques such as indexing, query optimization, and database schema design can improve the efficiency of data retrieval and storage operations.

Code profiling is another valuable technique for performance optimization. By analyzing your code's execution and identifying performance bottlenecks, you can make targeted optimizations to improve efficiency. Profiling tools can help pinpoint areas of code that consume excessive resources or contribute to slow performance.

To continuously monitor and optimize performance, leverage performance monitoring tools. These tools provide insights into application performance metrics, such as response times, CPU and memory usage, and database query performance. Monitoring allows you to identify performance degradation, detect anomalies, and take proactive measures to maintain optimal performance.

Development Efficiency and Developer Experience

In the fast-paced world of startups, development efficiency and a positive developer experience are essential for productivity and overall success. By prioritizing these factors, you can streamline your development workflow and create a conducive environment for innovation and collaboration.

Explore tools, libraries, and frameworks that promote code reusability and automation of repetitive tasks. Adopting technologies that facilitate efficient collaboration, such as version control systems and project management tools, can enhance team productivity.

Embracing development best practices, such as modular and clean code architecture, unit testing, and continuous integration and delivery processes, can further improve development efficiency. These practices ensure that your team can iterate quickly, identify and fix issues early on, and deliver high-quality software.

Investing in developer experience goes beyond providing the necessary tools and processes. It involves creating a positive and supportive work culture that encourages learning, growth, and experimentation. Foster a collaborative environment where developers can share knowledge, provide feedback, and contribute to the overall success of the startup.

By prioritizing development efficiency and developer experience, you empower your team to work effectively and efficiently, leading to faster development cycles, improved product quality, and increased innovation within your startup.

****

Selecting the appropriate tech stack is a pivotal step in establishing a strong technical foundation for your startup. Through a thoughtful evaluation of technologies and frameworks, considering crucial factors like scalability, performance, and development efficiency, you can position your startup for success. By choosing the right tools and technologies, you lay the groundwork for building a robust and scalable product.

Later, we will delve into the process of building a minimum viable product (MVP). This iterative approach allows you to validate your assumptions, gather feedback from users, and refine your product based on real-world insights. By continuously iterating and improving your product, you increase your chances of meeting market demands and delivering value to your target audience.

Remember, selecting a tech stack is not a one-time decision. As your startup evolves and grows, you may need to adapt and incorporate new technologies to meet changing requirements. Stay abreast of industry trends and advancements to ensure that your tech stack remains relevant and aligned with your startup's vision.

By making informed decisions about your tech stack and continuously refining your product, you can navigate the challenges of the startup landscape and position your venture for long-term success.

Chapter 5
Building the Tech Foundation

In the world of startups, a strong tech foundation is the bedrock for success. This chapter will take you on a journey through the essential elements of building a solid tech foundation for your venture. We will explore the fundamental principles of software architecture, scalability, performance, as well as the crucial aspects of security and data privacy. By understanding and implementing these key considerations, you'll be well-prepared to create a robust and reliable technological infrastructure that can support your startup's growth and ambitions. So, let's dive in and discover the building blocks that will lay the groundwork for your startup's technological success.

Software Architecture and Design Principles

Understanding Software Architecture

Software architecture is a critical aspect of building robust and scalable applications. It involves designing the structure and organization of a software system to meet specific requirements and achieve desired outcomes. By understanding software architecture, startups can create applications that are scalable, maintainable, and aligned with their business goals.

Start by exploring the fundamental concepts of software architecture. Gain insights into architectural patterns such as monolithic, microservices, and serverless architectures. Each pattern has its advantages and considerations, which can significantly impact the scalability, flexibility, and development process of your application.

Consider the unique requirements of your startup when selecting an architecture. Evaluate factors such as scalability goals, expected traffic, development team size, and future expansion plans. The chosen architecture should align with your startup's business objectives and support its growth trajectory.

For example, a monolithic architecture is suitable for smaller applications with straightforward functionality and lower scalability requirements. On the other hand, microservices architecture allows for modular development, scalability, and independent deployment of components. Serverless architecture enables automatic scaling and cost optimization by abstracting the underlying infrastructure.

By understanding software architecture and selecting the appropriate pattern for your startup, you can lay a strong foundation for building scalable and maintainable applications that can evolve and adapt to your business needs.

Design Principles for Sustainable Development

Design principles play a crucial role in developing software that is clean, modular, and maintainable. By adhering to these principles, startups can create codebases that are flexible, scalable, and easier to manage and evolve over time.

One essential design principle is the separation of concerns, which advocates for dividing a system into distinct modules, each responsible for a specific aspect of functionality. This promotes code modularity, making it easier to understand, test, and modify individual components without affecting the entire system.

The single responsibility principle emphasizes that each module or class should have a single responsibility or reason to change. By keeping code focused and cohesive, it becomes more readable, maintainable, and less prone to bugs. This principle encourages the creation of smaller, specialized components that can be easily reused and tested.

Dependency inversion is another important principle that promotes loose coupling between modules. It suggests that high-level modules should depend on abstractions rather than concrete implementations. This allows for easier swapping of dependencies and promotes flexibility and extensibility.

In addition to these principles, startups can benefit from applying design patterns, which are proven solutions to recurring software design problems. Design patterns provide standardized approaches to solving common challenges and help create scalable and maintainable code.

To ensure sustainable development, embrace coding best practices and coding standards. Follow consistent naming conventions, use meaningful comments, and adopt a modular and readable coding style. Regularly review and refactor your codebase to eliminate duplication, improve performance, and maintain a clean and efficient codebase.

By incorporating these design principles and best practices, startups can build software that is not only functional but also adaptable, maintainable, and capable of scaling to meet future needs.

Documentation and Communication

Documentation and communication are vital aspects of software development that enable effective collaboration within development teams. By documenting your architecture, design decisions, and technical specifications, you provide a reference for your team and future developers, ensuring a shared understanding of the system.

Start by creating architectural diagrams that illustrate the high-level structure of your software, including components, dependencies, and interfaces. Document the rationale behind your design decisions, explaining the trade-offs and considerations that influenced your choices.

Technical documentation should cover APIs, data models, configuration settings, and any other relevant information that developers need to understand and interact with the system. Clearly define interfaces, document usage examples, and provide code samples where necessary.

Communication tools and techniques are crucial for maintaining effective collaboration. Conduct regular code reviews to ensure code quality, identify potential issues, and share knowledge among team members. Architectural reviews can help validate design decisions and ensure adherence to best practices.

Team meetings, both synchronous and asynchronous, allow for discussions, brainstorming, and clarifications. Utilize collaboration platforms, chat tools, and project management software to facilitate communication and task coordination.

By documenting your tech foundation and fostering effective communication, you create a shared understanding within your team. This facilitates future enhancements, maintenance, and onboarding of new team members. Regularly update and maintain your documentation as the system evolves, ensuring its accuracy and usefulness over time.

Scalability and Performance Considerations

Scalability Strategies for Growing Startups

Scalability is a crucial consideration for startups aiming to accommodate growing user demands and scale their business effectively. By implementing appropriate scalability strategies, you can ensure your system can handle increased traffic, maintain performance, and deliver a seamless user experience.

One common approach to scalability is horizontal scaling, which involves adding more instances of your application to distribute the workload. This can be achieved through techniques like load balancing and auto-scaling, where resources are dynamically allocated based on demand. Vertical scaling, on the other hand, involves upgrading your existing infrastructure to handle increased loads by adding more powerful hardware.

Sharding is another technique that involves distributing data across multiple databases or servers to improve performance and scalability. By partitioning data based on specific criteria, you can distribute the workload and reduce the strain on individual components.

Caching is an effective strategy for improving performance and reducing the load on your backend systems. By caching frequently accessed data or computationally expensive results, you can serve them quickly without requiring repeated processing.

To ensure the scalability of your startup, it's essential to conduct load testing to simulate real-world traffic and identify potential bottlenecks. Performance optimization techniques, such as database optimization, code optimization, and caching, can help improve the efficiency of your system and enhance scalability.

By designing your architecture to be inherently scalable, leveraging technologies that enable automatic scaling, and regularly optimizing performance, you can ensure that your startup can handle increasing user demands, maintain excellent user experience, and support future growth.

Performance Optimization Techniques

Optimizing performance is key to providing a fast and responsive user experience, which can significantly impact user satisfaction and retention. By implementing various performance optimization techniques, you can improve the speed and efficiency of your application.

One area to focus on is optimizing database queries. By analyzing query performance, indexing the right fields, and avoiding unnecessary database operations, you can significantly reduce the response time and improve overall system performance. Caching mechanisms, such as in-memory caching or content caching, can help store frequently accessed data, reducing the need for repetitive database queries and improving response times.

Reducing network latency is another crucial aspect of performance optimization. Leveraging content delivery networks (CDNs) allows you to distribute your static assets across multiple servers worldwide, enabling users to access them from a location closer to them. Additionally, compressing files, optimizing network protocols, and minimizing the use of external resources can further reduce network latency and improve overall performance.

Efficient resource utilization is essential for optimal performance. This includes optimizing code to minimize CPU and memory usage, implementing efficient algorithms and data structures, and leveraging asynchronous processing to handle concurrent requests.

Monitoring and analyzing performance metrics are vital to identifying bottlenecks and areas for improvement. By using monitoring tools and analyzing metrics such as response time, throughput, and error rates, you can pinpoint performance issues and take proactive steps to optimize your tech foundation.

Regular performance testing and benchmarking can help validate the effectiveness of your optimization efforts and ensure that your startup is delivering optimal performance to users.

By optimizing database queries, improving caching mechanisms, reducing network latency, ensuring efficient resource utilization, and continuously monitoring performance metrics, you can enhance the performance of your application and provide users with a seamless and satisfying experience.

Balancing Performance and Cost Efficiency

Achieving a balance between performance and cost efficiency is crucial for startups aiming to optimize their resources while delivering a satisfactory user experience. Here are some strategies to help you strike this balance:

Cost-Effective Scaling: When scaling your infrastructure, consider cost-effective options such as horizontal scaling, which involves adding more servers or instances, as it can be more affordable than vertical scaling. Explore cloud service providers that offer flexible pricing models and scalability features to align with your budget and scaling needs.

Performance Monitoring and Optimization: Continuously monitor the performance of your application and identify areas for optimization. Prioritize optimization efforts on critical components that significantly impact user experience. By focusing on specific bottlenecks, you can achieve performance improvements without incurring unnecessary costs.

Efficient Resource Utilization: Optimize the utilization of your resources to reduce costs. This can include techniques such as optimizing database queries, implementing caching mechanisms, and using efficient algorithms and data structures to minimize computational and memory requirements.

Technology Evaluation: When making technology investments, consider the long-term costs associated with maintenance, support, and licensing fees. Evaluate open-source alternatives or technologies with flexible pricing options that align with your startup's financial resources.

Cost Optimization through Automation: Explore automation tools and processes that streamline development, deployment, and infrastructure management. Automation can reduce manual effort, increase efficiency, and ultimately lead to cost savings.

Prioritize Performance-Driven Features: Understand your users' needs and prioritize the features and functionalities that directly contribute to performance and user experience. This ensures that you allocate resources effectively and focus on areas that provide the most value.

By consistently evaluating the cost implications of scaling and optimization strategies, making informed technology choices, and prioritizing performance improvements based on user needs, you can strike a balance between performance and cost efficiency, maximizing the value of your resources while meeting user expectations.

Security and Data Privacy Best Practices

Securing Your Tech Foundation

Ensuring the security of your tech foundation is crucial to protect your startup and its users from potential threats and vulnerabilities. Here are some best practices to help you secure your tech foundation:

Threat Awareness: Understand common security threats and vulnerabilities, such as cross-site scripting (XSS), SQL injection, and cross-site request forgery (CSRF). Stay informed about emerging threats to proactively mitigate risks.

Authentication and Authorization: Implement robust authentication mechanisms, such as multi-factor authentication (MFA) and secure password policies. Use secure authorization protocols to control access to sensitive resources and ensure proper user permissions.

Secure Communication: Utilize secure communication protocols, such as HTTPS, to encrypt data transmission between your application and users. Protect sensitive data in transit by implementing secure socket layer (SSL) or transport layer security (TLS) encryption.

Data Encryption: Apply encryption techniques to protect sensitive data at rest, such as customer information or login credentials stored in databases. Utilize strong encryption algorithms and manage encryption keys securely.

Secure Coding Practices: Follow secure coding practices, including input validation, output encoding, and parameterized queries to prevent common vulnerabilities like injection attacks. Regularly update and patch your software dependencies to address known security vulnerabilities.

Regular Security Audits: Conduct periodic security audits and penetration testing to identify vulnerabilities and weaknesses in your tech foundation. Fix any identified issues promptly and establish a process for ongoing security testing and monitoring.

Stay Updated on Security Trends: Keep abreast of the latest security trends, vulnerabilities, and best practices. Participate in security communities and forums, follow security blogs, and leverage security tools and services to enhance your security posture.

By implementing these security practices, you can enhance the resilience of your tech foundation and safeguard your startup from potential breaches. Prioritize security from the outset and adopt a proactive approach to identify and address security risks to maintain the trust of your users and protect your valuable assets.

Data Privacy and Compliance

Data privacy and compliance are of utmost importance in today's digital landscape. As a startup, it is crucial to prioritize these aspects to build trust with your customers and maintain regulatory adherence. Failure to safeguard user data can lead to significant consequences, including reputational damage and legal ramifications.

First and foremost, it is essential to have a thorough understanding of data privacy principles. Transparency, purpose limitation, data minimization, and accountability are some of the fundamental principles that guide responsible data collection, processing, and storage practices. By adhering to these principles, you can ensure that your startup collects and uses user data in a lawful and ethical manner.

Compliance with data protection regulations is another crucial aspect. Depending on your jurisdiction and industry, there may be specific regulations that you need to comply with, such as the GDPR or industry-specific guidelines. It is important to familiarize yourself with the requirements and obligations imposed by these regulations and take the necessary steps to meet them. This may include appointing a data protection officer, conducting privacy impact assessments, and implementing privacy-by-design principles.

Anonymization of data is an effective technique to protect user privacy. By removing personally identifiable information from the data you collect, you can ensure that it cannot be linked back to individuals. This is particularly important when sharing or analyzing data for research or other purposes.

Secure data storage is paramount to protecting user data from unauthorized access and breaches. Encryption, access controls, and strong authentication mechanisms should be implemented to safeguard data at rest and in transit. Regular security assessments and updates to security protocols are essential to address any vulnerabilities and stay one step ahead of potential threats.

Obtaining explicit user consent is crucial for data collection and processing activities. Users should be provided with clear information on how their data will be used and the ability to manage their preferences. It is important to implement user-friendly consent mechanisms and ensure that users have control over their data.

Privacy by design should be integrated into your product development process. From the early stages, privacy considerations should be embedded into the design and architecture of your tech foundation. By implementing privacy controls and safeguards at the core of your product, you can ensure that privacy is not an afterthought but a fundamental aspect of your startup.

Additionally, startups should establish data retention policies and regularly review and delete data that is no longer necessary.

This helps to minimize data storage and reduce the risk of unauthorized access. Having processes in place to respond to user data deletion requests is also crucial to meet regulatory requirements and respect user rights.

Training and awareness among your team members are vital for maintaining data privacy and compliance. Your employees should be educated on data privacy best practices, their responsibilities in handling user data, and the potential risks associated with non-compliance. Regular training sessions and updates on emerging privacy concerns are essential to keep your team informed and proactive in protecting user data.

By prioritizing data privacy and compliance, startups can establish themselves as trustworthy entities that respect user privacy rights. Implementing robust privacy measures, maintaining transparency in data handling, and fostering a culture of privacy within the organization are all key steps towards building a strong foundation for long-term success.

****

Establishing a strong tech foundation is vital for the success and sustainability of your startup. By comprehending software architecture, adopting sound design principles, and prioritizing scalability, performance, security, and data privacy, you can build a reliable and robust foundation for your startup's growth.

Understanding software architecture allows you to select the most suitable architectural pattern for your startup, considering its unique requirements and business objectives. By adhering to design principles that promote clean and maintainable code, you ensure the longevity and scalability of your codebase.

Scalability and performance considerations enable your startup to handle increasing user demands and deliver a fast and responsive user experience. Implementing scalability strategies and performance optimization techniques allows your application to scale seamlessly and optimize resource usage.

Security and data privacy are essential in today's digital landscape. By implementing robust security measures, adhering to data protection regulations, and prioritizing user privacy, you build trust with your customers and protect sensitive data from unauthorized access or breaches.

By laying a solid tech foundation, you establish a reliable and secure platform for your startup's operations. This not only ensures a seamless user experience but also provides a solid base for future growth and innovation.

Chapter 6
Developing a Minimum Viable Product (MVP)

Building a Minimum Viable Product (MVP) is a pivotal stage in the startup journey. By adopting an iterative development approach and leveraging agile practices, startups can validate their ideas, gather user feedback, and iterate based on market response. Focusing on delivering the essential functionality, startups can minimize development time and costs while gaining valuable insights from early users.

Additionally, we will discuss the importance of implementing feedback loops and user testing throughout the development process. By gathering and analyzing user feedback, startups can refine their product, improve user experience, and align with market needs.

By following these principles and practices, startups can accelerate their product development, mitigate risks, and increase the chances of success in the market. Let's dive in and discover the strategies for building a compelling and market-ready product.

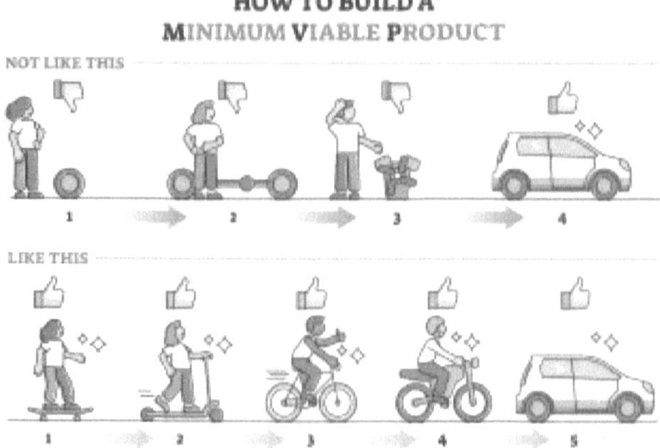

Iterative Development and Agile Practices

Understanding Iterative Development

Traditional waterfall development approaches may prove too rigid and slow to meet evolving market demands. This is where iterative development comes into play. Iterative development is a flexible methodology that focuses on delivering software in incremental stages, allowing for continuous feedback and improvement.

By breaking the development process into smaller iterations, startups can quickly gather user feedback and incorporate changes throughout the project lifecycle. This iterative approach enables them to adapt to shifting market needs, validate assumptions, and refine their product in real-time.

One of the key principles of iterative development is rapid feedback. By releasing a functional product iteration early on, startups can obtain valuable insights from users, stakeholders, and market trends. This feedback serves as a foundation for making informed decisions, optimizing the product's features, and prioritizing future iterations.

Agile methodologies, such as Scrum or Kanban, provide frameworks for implementing iterative development practices. Scrum, for example, emphasizes close collaboration within cross-functional teams, time-boxed iterations (sprints), and frequent communication through daily stand-up meetings. Kanban, on the other hand, visualizes the workflow and promotes a continuous flow of tasks, allowing teams to respond quickly to changing priorities.

Embracing an iterative development mindset brings several benefits to startups. Firstly, it reduces the time to market by enabling the release of a minimum viable product (MVP) sooner, allowing for faster user feedback and validation. It also enhances adaptability, as startups can respond promptly to market shifts and customer needs. Furthermore, the incremental nature of iterative development enables continuous improvement, ensuring that the product evolves in line with user expectations and business goals.

Agile Development Practices for Startups

Adopting agile development practices can be a game-changer. Agile methodologies offer a flexible and iterative approach to building software, enabling startups to adapt quickly to market feedback and deliver value to their users.

One of the fundamental agile practices is the use of user stories. User stories capture user requirements and goals in a concise format, enabling you to prioritize features and align your development efforts with user needs. By breaking down complex functionalities into smaller, manageable pieces, you can deliver incremental value to your users.

Sprints, another vital agile practice, divide the development process into short, time-boxed iterations. Each sprint focuses on delivering a specific set of user stories, allowing you to continuously iterate and improve your product. Daily stand-up meetings keep your team aligned, fostering communication and enabling timely issue resolution.

Retrospectives provide an opportunity to reflect on the development process, celebrate successes, and identify areas for improvement. By regularly evaluating your team's performance and learning from past experiences, you can continuously enhance your development practices.

Embracing a "fail fast, learn fast" mindset is crucial in the startup world. It encourages experimentation and quick iterations, enabling you to gather valuable feedback and make data-driven decisions. This iterative approach empowers startups to deliver high-quality products that meet user needs efficiently.

To streamline your development workflow, leverage tools and automation. Project management software, version control systems, and continuous integration/delivery pipelines automate repetitive tasks, enhance collaboration, and ensure the stability of your codebase.

Creating an MVP Roadmap and Prioritizing Features

Defining Your MVP Vision

In the startup journey, defining a clear vision for your Minimum Viable Product (MVP) is essential. To start, it's crucial to identify the problem you're solving and articulate your value proposition. What pain points are you addressing? How will your product provide a unique solution? By clearly defining the problem and the value your product brings, you can align your efforts with the needs of your target audience.

Next, it's important to identify the core features that will deliver the most value to your users. These features should address the critical pain points and provide a meaningful experience. Remember, the focus of an MVP is to provide the minimum functionality required to validate your product idea and gather user feedback.

Understanding the concept of the "minimum" in MVP is vital. It means finding the right balance between delivering functionality and keeping the scope minimal. The goal is to create a product that is viable for user testing and validation, without adding unnecessary complexity or features that can delay the development process. By defining your MVP vision with clarity and purpose, you set the stage for building a product that resonates with your target audience and provides tangible value.

Prioritizing Features

In the process of building your Minimum Viable Product (MVP), prioritizing features is a crucial step. One commonly used technique is the MoSCoW method, which categorizes features into four priority levels: Must-haves, Should-haves, Could-haves, and Won't-haves. Must-haves represent essential features that are critical to solving the user's problem and delivering value. Should-haves are important but not critical, while Could-haves are nice-to-have features that can enhance the user experience. Won't-haves are intentionally excluded from the MVP.

Another technique is the impact-effort matrix, which assesses the impact of a feature on user satisfaction or business goals against the effort required to implement it. This matrix helps you prioritize features based on their potential impact and the resources required for development.

User story mapping is another valuable technique that allows you to visually organize and prioritize features based on user journeys. By breaking down features into user stories and arranging them in a logical flow, you can identify the core functionalities needed to provide value to your users.

When prioritizing features, consider factors such as user feedback, market demand, technical feasibility, and alignment with your business goals. Strive to strike a balance between delivering a compelling user experience and managing the development efforts within the constraints of time, resources, and scope.

By effectively prioritizing features, you can ensure that your MVP focuses on the most critical user needs and delivers value to your target audience. This approach allows you to gather valuable feedback, iterate on your product, and incrementally add features in subsequent iterations, increasing the chances of building a successful and sustainable startup.

Creating an MVP Roadmap

Creating a roadmap for your Minimum Viable Product (MVP) is essential to guide the development process and ensure a clear direction.

Start by breaking down the features identified in the previous section into actionable tasks. Define the specific activities and deliverables required to implement each feature. This breakdown allows for better estimation of effort, resources, and dependencies.

Next, establish a timeline for your MVP development. Consider factors such as the complexity of features, availability of resources, and any external dependencies. Be realistic in your timeline estimation, allowing for unforeseen challenges and iterations.

Communicate the roadmap with your development team and stakeholders. Transparency and alignment are crucial to manage expectations and ensure everyone is on the same page. By sharing the roadmap, you foster collaboration and provide visibility into the development process.

Regularly review and update the roadmap as the development progresses. As you gather user feedback and iterate on your MVP, adjust the roadmap to incorporate new insights and priorities. A flexible roadmap allows for adaptation and ensures that your MVP stays aligned with your evolving understanding of user needs.

Remember that the MVP roadmap is not set in stone. It serves as a guide but should be adaptable to changes and discoveries along the development journey. Stay agile and be open to adjustments that improve the value and usability of your product.

By creating an MVP roadmap, you establish a clear plan for developing and refining your product. This roadmap helps manage resources, set expectations, and provide a roadmap for future iterations and enhancements. It serves as a valuable tool to keep your team and stakeholders aligned and focused on delivering a successful MVP.

Feedback Loops and User Testing for Continuous Improvement

Gathering User Feedback

Gathering user feedback is a crucial step in the iterative development process of your Minimum Viable Product (MVP). One of the most direct ways to gather user feedback is through user surveys and interviews. Design targeted surveys to collect specific insights about user preferences, pain points, and satisfaction levels. Conduct interviews with representative users to gain deeper insights and uncover valuable qualitative feedback.

Usability testing is another powerful method to gather feedback. Create realistic scenarios and observe how users interact with your product. Pay attention to their actions, frustrations, and suggestions. Usability testing can reveal usability issues, user experience gaps, and potential areas for improvement.

Analyzing analytics data is also essential for understanding user behavior. Track key metrics, such as user engagement, conversion rates, and retention. Identify patterns, trends, and user flow bottlenecks to gain insights into how users are using your product.

To encourage user feedback, establish channels where users can easily provide their input. Implement feedback forms within your product, set up customer support channels, or create a community forum where users can share their ideas and suggestions.

Remember to actively listen to your users and empathize with their pain points and needs. Their feedback is a valuable source of information that can guide your product enhancements. Prioritize and categorize user feedback based on its impact and feasibility for implementation.

By gathering user feedback, you gain valuable insights that can inform your product roadmap and future iterations. Act upon the feedback by addressing pain points, improving user experience, and adding features that align with user needs. This iterative feedback loop ensures that your MVP evolves based on real user input, leading to a more successful and user-centric product.

Implementing User Testing

User testing involves observing real users interacting with your product and gathering feedback on their experiences. This process helps validate assumptions, uncover usability issues, and gather valuable insights to inform product improvements.

One popular technique is usability testing, where you provide users with specific tasks to complete while observing their interactions. This approach allows you to identify areas where users may struggle, encounter confusion, or experience difficulties. By directly observing user behavior, you can uncover usability issues and make informed decisions to enhance the user experience.

A/B testing is another powerful method for user testing. It involves presenting users with different versions of your product or specific features to compare their performance and gather quantitative data on user preferences. A/B testing helps you make data-driven decisions by analyzing user behavior and preferences.

Heatmaps and session recordings are additional tools that can provide valuable insights. Heatmaps visualize user interactions, highlighting areas of interest, clicks, and scrolling patterns. Session recordings capture user interactions, allowing you to review and analyze user behavior firsthand.

Throughout the user testing process, it's crucial to gather both qualitative and quantitative data. Collect feedback from users through surveys, interviews, or feedback forms to gain insights into their preferences, pain points, and suggestions. Combine this feedback with quantitative data to form a comprehensive understanding of user behavior and preferences.

Iterate based on the user feedback and insights gained from the testing process. Make informed decisions to refine and improve your product, addressing usability issues, enhancing user experience, and aligning with user expectations.

By implementing user testing, you ensure that your MVP is validated by real users, leading to a more user-centric and successful product. Use the insights gained from user testing to drive continuous improvement and create a product that meets the needs and expectations of your target audience.

Continuous Improvement and Iteration

Continuous improvement and iteration are vital for the success of your startup and the long-term evolution of your product. To drive continuous improvement, it's essential to create an environment that encourages learning from failures and values experimentation. Embrace the concept of "fail fast, learn fast" to encourage your team to take risks, try new ideas, and iterate quickly based on feedback. Emphasize the importance of learning from setbacks and using those lessons to inform future decisions.

Cross-functional collaboration is key in fostering continuous improvement. Encourage close collaboration between developers, designers, and product managers to identify areas of improvement and leverage their diverse perspectives. By bringing together different skill sets and viewpoints, you can uncover innovative solutions and drive meaningful enhancements.

Implementing a feedback loop is crucial for continuous improvement. Establish channels for gathering user feedback, such as customer support channels, feedback forms, or user community forums. Actively listen to your users, analyze their feedback, and prioritize the most impactful changes based on their needs and pain points. Embrace an iterative development process that allows for quick deployment of updates and improvements based on user feedback.

Regularly reassess your product roadmap and adapt based on user feedback, market changes, and emerging technologies.

Continuously challenge assumptions and validate your product's value proposition in the evolving market landscape. Stay informed about industry trends and leverage emerging technologies to enhance your product and maintain a competitive edge.

By embracing a culture of continuous improvement and iteration, you empower your team to drive innovation, respond to user needs, and deliver a high-quality product. Through constant learning, adaptation, and leveraging user feedback, you can ensure that your startup evolves and thrives in a dynamic market.

****

Developing a Minimum Viable Product (MVP) is a crucial step in the startup journey. By understanding the iterative development approach, prioritizing features, and implementing feedback loops, you can create a product that meets user needs and drives continuous improvement. The ability to adapt and iterate based on user feedback is key to building a successful startup.

We explored the importance of defining the MVP vision, prioritizing features, creating an MVP roadmap, gathering user feedback, implementing user testing, and embracing continuous improvement and iteration. These practices are essential for building a product that delivers value, meets user expectations, and evolves with the changing market dynamics.

As you embark on your MVP journey, remember to stay agile, listen to your users, and be open to making adjustments based on their feedback. The goal is to create a product that solves a real problem, delivers value, and sets the foundation for future growth.

Chapter 7
Leveraging the Power of the Cloud

Cloud computing has become a game-changer, providing startups with the tools and resources needed to scale, innovate, and thrive in today's digital landscape.

We will begin by understanding the foundational principles of cloud computing. We'll explore concepts such as on-demand self-service, resource pooling, and rapid elasticity, gaining a solid understanding of how the cloud works and its benefits for startups.

Next, we'll dive into the remarkable advantages that cloud computing brings to startups. From cost savings and scalability to global accessibility and enhanced collaboration, the cloud offers a host of benefits that can drive your startup's growth and success.

We'll then explore the wide range of cloud infrastructure and platform services available to startups. Whether it's virtual machines, containers, serverless computing, or managed databases, we'll discuss the various options and their use cases, helping you make informed decisions for your startup.

Deploying your applications effectively in the cloud is crucial for success. We'll discuss best practices and deployment strategies to ensure high availability, fault tolerance, and scalability. You'll learn how to design and manage your startup's infrastructure to meet the demands of your growing user base.

Lastly, we'll delve into cost optimization techniques in the cloud. While the cloud offers immense potential, managing costs is essential. We'll explore strategies to optimize spending, monitor usage, and leverage cost-effective resources, helping you make the most of your cloud investment.

By the end of this chapter, you'll have a comprehensive understanding of cloud computing and how it can empower your startup with scalability, efficiency, and cost-effectiveness. So let's dive in and discover the world of cloud technologies for startups.

Unveiling the Essence of Cloud Computing

An Insight into Cloud Computing

To embark on our exploration of cloud computing, let us unravel its essence and understand its fundamental principles. By distinguishing between traditional on-premises infrastructure and cloud-based solutions, we can grasp the transformative power that cloud computing bestows upon startups.

Cloud computing represents a paradigm shift in the way resources are provisioned and consumed. Unlike traditional infrastructure, which requires upfront investment and maintenance, cloud computing offers a flexible and scalable approach. With cloud solutions, startups can access computing power, storage, and services on-demand, paying only for what they use.

One of the defining characteristics of cloud computing is self-service provisioning. Startups can easily spin up resources and configure them as needed, eliminating the need for manual intervention and reducing time to market. This self-service nature empowers startups to rapidly scale their infrastructure based on their evolving needs.

Resource pooling is another key aspect of cloud computing. Cloud providers consolidate their resources to serve multiple customers, enabling startups to benefit from shared infrastructure. This pooling allows for efficient utilization of resources and better cost optimization.

Elasticity is a crucial feature offered by cloud computing. Startups can dynamically scale their resources up or down based on demand. This scalability ensures that the infrastructure can handle sudden spikes in traffic without compromising performance or incurring unnecessary costs during periods of low demand.

Utility-based billing is a fundamental principle of cloud computing. Startups pay for the resources they consume, similar to how we pay for utilities like electricity or water. This pay-as-you-go model enables startups to align their costs with their usage, promoting cost-efficiency and financial flexibility.

Public clouds offer services and infrastructure accessible to the general public, providing a cost-effective and scalable solution. Private clouds, on the other hand, are dedicated to a single organization, offering enhanced control and security. Hybrid clouds combine the benefits of both public and private clouds, allowing startups to leverage the advantages of each model based on their specific requirements.

By delving into the essence of cloud computing and understanding its defining principles, we can unlock its full potential for startups.

Embracing the Benefits of Cloud Computing for Startups

In our exploration of cloud computing, it is crucial to fully embrace the profound advantages it offers to startups, fueling their growth and success. Scalability is a game-changer for startups. Cloud computing allows startups to easily scale their infrastructure to accommodate increasing user demands. Whether it's handling sudden traffic spikes or expanding to new markets, the cloud provides the agility to scale up or down as needed, ensuring a seamless user experience.

Flexibility is another key benefit of the cloud. Startups can quickly adapt to changing business requirements by leveraging the vast array of services and resources available. With the ability to provision and configure resources on-demand, startups can experiment, iterate, and pivot with ease, enabling them to stay ahead of the competition.

Time to market is crucial for startups, and the cloud significantly accelerates the development and deployment process. By providing ready-to-use infrastructure and platform services, the cloud eliminates the need for startups to build everything from scratch. This rapid access to resources allows startups to focus on developing their core product or service, reducing time to market and gaining a competitive edge.

From a financial perspective, cloud computing offers significant cost-saving potential. Startups can avoid substantial upfront hardware investments and the associated maintenance costs. Instead, they can leverage the pay-as-you-go model, paying only for the resources they consume. This cost optimization allows startups to allocate their financial resources more efficiently, investing in innovation and growth rather than infrastructure overhead.

Moreover, startups can offload the complexities of infrastructure management and maintenance. This empowers them to focus on their core competencies, nurturing innovation and differentiation. With the cloud handling infrastructure-related tasks, startups can redirect their valuable time and resources towards delivering exceptional products and services to their customers.

By fully embracing the benefits of cloud computing, startups can leverage its scalability, flexibility, accelerated time to market, and cost-saving advantages. This enables them to propel their growth, stay competitive in the market, and create a solid foundation for success.

Expanding Horizons with Cloud Infrastructure and Platform Services

Embracing Infrastructure as a Service (IaaS)

Infrastructure as a Service (IaaS), a foundational cloud computing model that revolutionizes how startups access and manage their computing resources. IaaS enables startups to leverage virtualized computing resources, such as virtual machines, storage, and networks, delivered over the internet.

With IaaS, startups can embrace the freedom and flexibility of cloud computing. Rather than investing in and maintaining physical infrastructure, they can rely on IaaS providers to provision and manage the underlying infrastructure. This allows startups to focus their energy and resources on their core business objectives.

One of the key advantages of IaaS is scalability. Startups can effortlessly scale their infrastructure up or down based on their changing needs. Whether it's handling increased user traffic, expanding into new markets, or accommodating seasonal fluctuations, IaaS offers the agility to allocate computing resources as needed. This scalability ensures that startups can deliver a seamless user experience, even during peak demand periods.

Additionally, IaaS provides startups with the opportunity to access enterprise-grade infrastructure without the associated costs and complexities. By leveraging IaaS offerings from cloud providers, startups can tap into robust and reliable computing resources that are maintained and managed by experts. This eliminates the need for upfront hardware investments and ongoing infrastructure maintenance, allowing startups to allocate their resources more efficiently.

Furthermore, IaaS offers startups the ability to quickly prototype, experiment, and innovate. With virtualized environments and readily available resources, startups can rapidly spin up new instances, test new ideas, and iterate on their products or services. This agility fosters innovation and enables startups to stay ahead in the competitive landscape.

By embracing IaaS, startups can unlock the power of virtualized computing resources, enabling them to scale their infrastructure, respond to changing demands, and focus on their core business objectives.

Unleashing the Power of Platform as a Service (PaaS)

Let us now delve into the remarkable capabilities of Platform as a Service (PaaS), a cloud computing model that elevates startups' ability to focus on application development and innovation. PaaS provides a pre-configured platform, complete with development tools, frameworks, and runtime environments, enabling startups to streamline the software development lifecycle.

With PaaS, startups can unleash their creativity and productivity by leveraging ready-to-use development platforms. These platforms eliminate the need for startups to worry about infrastructure setup, software installation, or system configuration. Instead, they can focus on writing code, designing applications, and delivering value to their customers.

One of the key advantages of PaaS is the speed and efficiency it brings to the development process. Startups can quickly provision and deploy their applications onto the PaaS platform, leveraging the built-in services and tools that simplify tasks like database management, security, and scalability. This reduces the time and effort required for development, allowing startups to iterate rapidly and deliver products or services to market faster.

Furthermore, PaaS promotes collaboration and teamwork within startup environments. Development teams can easily share code, collaborate on projects, and integrate their work seamlessly. The centralized platform provides a unified environment where developers can work together, leveraging version control systems, collaboration tools, and continuous integration and deployment pipelines.

By embracing PaaS, startups can achieve enhanced productivity, faster time to market, and streamlined collaboration. With the infrastructure and development platform abstracted away, startups can focus on their core competencies and drive innovation. PaaS empowers startups to deliver exceptional products and services with agility, giving them a competitive edge in the market.

Maximizing the Benefits: Deployment Strategies and Cost Optimization

Strategic Deployment in the Cloud

As you embark on deploying your startup's infrastructure in the cloud, it's crucial to navigate the intricacies and choose the right deployment strategies.

Virtual machines (VMs) offer a tried-and-true deployment option, providing isolated and customizable environments for your applications. By leveraging VMs, startups can run multiple instances of their applications on a shared physical server, enabling efficient resource utilization and easy scaling. VMs also allow startups to maintain control over the operating system, runtime environment, and software dependencies.

Containers, on the other hand, provide a lightweight and portable deployment option. With containerization technologies like Docker and Kubernetes, startups can package their applications and their dependencies into self-contained units. Containers offer flexibility, enabling easy deployment and scaling across different cloud environments and reducing potential compatibility issues. They also promote faster application deployment and rapid iteration cycles.

Another innovative deployment approach is serverless architecture. With serverless computing, startups can focus solely on writing and deploying code without the need to provision or manage underlying infrastructure. Functions are executed on-demand, scaling automatically based on the incoming workload. Serverless architectures offer cost-effectiveness by charging only for actual usage and eliminating idle resource costs.

When designing your deployment strategy, it's important to consider scalability, fault tolerance, and high availability. Cloud providers offer services like load balancers, auto-scaling groups, and distributed databases to handle fluctuations in user demand and ensure consistent performance. Designing your architecture to be resilient and fault-tolerant, with redundancy and failover mechanisms, will help minimize disruptions and maintain a seamless user experience.

Unveiling the Secrets of Cost Optimization

Optimizing cloud costs is essential for startups looking to maximize the value of their cloud investment. One key aspect of cost optimization is rightsizing resources. It involves analyzing the usage patterns of your applications and selecting the appropriate instance types, storage options, and network configurations that align with your workload requirements. By rightsizing your resources, you can avoid overprovisioning and underutilization, optimizing costs without sacrificing performance.

Another cost optimization technique is leveraging spot instances. Spot instances allow you to bid on spare computing capacity in the cloud, often available at significantly lower prices compared to on-demand instances. By using spot instances for non-critical or fault-tolerant workloads, startups can achieve substantial cost savings. However, it's important to consider the potential for instance termination when the spot price exceeds your bid, so it's recommended to have contingency plans in place.

Implementing autoscaling policies can also contribute to cost optimization. Autoscaling enables your infrastructure to automatically adjust its capacity based on demand. By dynamically scaling resources up during peak periods and scaling down during periods of low demand, you can optimize resource utilization and cost efficiency. Autoscaling can be applied to various cloud services, such as virtual machines, containers, and serverless functions.

Cloud cost management tools and services provided by cloud providers can be invaluable in optimizing costs. These tools offer insights into your cloud spending, enabling you to identify areas of overspending and make informed decisions to optimize costs. Additionally, you can set budget alerts and utilization thresholds to monitor your spending and take proactive measures to control costs.

Regularly reviewing and optimizing your cloud architecture and usage is crucial for ongoing cost optimization. As your startup evolves and grows, your cloud infrastructure needs may change. Continuously evaluating your resource allocation, decommissioning unused resources, and adopting cost-effective services or pricing models can help you optimize costs in the long term.

****

We embarked on a captivating exploration of cloud computing and its transformative power for startups. We delved into the foundational principles of cloud computing, distinguishing it from traditional on-premises infrastructure. We also explored the remarkable benefits that the cloud offers to startups, including scalability, flexibility, and cost-effectiveness. By leveraging Infrastructure as a Service (IaaS) and Platform as a Service (PaaS), startups can harness the full potential of the cloud, focusing on innovation and application development.

Additionally, we discussed strategic deployment strategies in the cloud, exploring virtual machines, containers, and serverless architectures. By designing resilient and fault-tolerant architectures, startups can ensure high availability and seamless user experiences. We also unveiled the secrets of cost optimization in the cloud, emphasizing rightsizing resources, leveraging spot instances, and implementing autoscaling policies to optimize costs without compromising performance.

Armed with these insights and techniques, your startup is well-equipped to leverage the power of the cloud, accelerating growth and success.

Chapter 8
Funding and Investment Strategies

Securing funding is a crucial step for startup founders in their journey towards success. Whether you choose to bootstrap your startup or seek external funding, understanding the options and approaches available to you is essential.

As a developer-founder, you bring a unique perspective to the table when approaching investors. We will explore how to leverage your technical expertise and showcase the potential of your product or technology to attract investment. From crafting a compelling pitch to identifying the right investors and negotiating deal terms, we will cover the key aspects of engaging with investors and securing the funding your startup needs.

By understanding the funding landscape and implementing proven strategies, you can increase your chances of obtaining the necessary resources to fuel your startup's growth.

Bootstrapping: Building from the Ground Up

When it comes to funding a startup, bootstrapping offers a unique approach that empowers founders to build their ventures with limited external resources. Bootstrapping involves relying on personal savings, generated revenue from the business, and resourcefulness to fund the growth of the startup.

Bootstrapping Strategies for Developer-Founders

Developer-founders have a unique advantage when it comes to bootstrapping their startups. Their technical skills and expertise allow them to adopt specific strategies that maximize cost efficiency and operational effectiveness.

One key strategy is cost minimization. Developer-founders can leverage their coding abilities to develop in-house solutions instead of relying on expensive third-party tools or services. By building their own software, they can significantly reduce costs while maintaining control over the development process.

Operational efficiency is another crucial aspect. Developer-founders can streamline workflows and automate repetitive tasks by implementing DevOps practices. By optimizing processes and eliminating inefficiencies, they can make the most of their limited resources and enhance productivity.

Leveraging open-source technologies is also a valuable approach for developer-founders. Open-source software provides cost-effective alternatives to proprietary solutions, enabling startups to leverage powerful tools and frameworks without incurring hefty licensing fees. Additionally, the open-source community often provides robust support and regular updates, ensuring the reliability and security of these technologies.

Real Life Example

One inspiring real-life example of a successful bootstrapped startup led by a developer-founder is Basecamp. Basecamp, a project management software company, was founded by Jason Fried and David Heinemeier Hansson. They initially started the company with their own savings and focused on building a simple, user-friendly product that catered to the needs of small businesses. By leveraging their development skills and employing efficient operational practices, they were able to grow the company organically without external funding.

Another notable example is MailChimp, an email marketing platform founded by Ben Chestnut and Dan Kurzius. They started the company with their own resources and gradually grew it by providing a reliable and user-friendly email marketing solution. By leveraging open-source technologies and implementing cost-effective marketing strategies, MailChimp was able to gain a significant market share and become a successful bootstrapped startup.

These examples demonstrate the power of bootstrapping for developer-founders. By focusing on cost minimization, operational efficiency, and leveraging open-source technologies, they were able to build successful businesses without relying on external funding. These strategies not only allowed them to overcome financial constraints but also enabled them to maintain control over their product and direction.

By adopting similar approaches and learning from the experiences of these successful bootstrapped startups, developer-founders can make the most of their technical expertise and resources, accelerating their startup's growth while maintaining financial independence.

Seeking External Funding

External funding can play a pivotal role in accelerating the growth of startups. From angel investors and venture capital firms to crowdfunding platforms and government grants, we delve into the various avenues through which startups can secure external funding.

Angel investors often bring valuable industry expertise, mentorship, and networking opportunities to the table. Venture capital firms, on the other hand, pool together funds from multiple investors to provide early-stage and growth-stage financing to startups. These firms not only offer financial support but also provide guidance, connections, and strategic advice.

Crowdfunding platforms have gained significant popularity in recent years. They allow startups to raise funds from a large number of individuals who contribute small amounts of money. This approach not only provides financial support but also enables startups to validate their ideas and build a community of early adopters and supporters.

Government grants are another funding option for startups, particularly in certain industries or regions. These grants are often provided to support innovation and economic development. Startups can leverage these grants to fund research and development, product development, or other specific projects.

When considering external funding, founders need to carefully weigh the advantages and considerations. Factors such as equity ownership, control over decision-making, access to expertise and networks, and long-term strategic alignment should be taken into account. It's essential to align with investors who share the startup's vision and can contribute value beyond financial support.

Approaching Investors as a Developer-Founder

Approaching investors as a developer-founder requires a tailored approach that effectively showcases your technical expertise and aligns with the investor's perspective. One key strategy is to articulate the market opportunities and the problem your startup is solving. Investors are interested in understanding the size of the market and the potential for growth. As a developer-founder, you can leverage your technical knowledge to demonstrate a deep understanding of the industry and how your solution addresses a significant pain point.

Building a compelling narrative around your product or service is crucial. Communicate the value proposition clearly and concisely, emphasizing how it solves a specific problem and offers a unique advantage.

GitHub, founded by Tom Preston-Werner, Chris Wanstrath, and PJ Hyett, secured funding by showcasing their technical expertise and understanding of the developer community. Investors recognized the potential of their platform for revolutionizing code collaboration and version control. Stripe, founded by Patrick and John Collison, leveraged their technical prowess and deep understanding of payment integration challenges. Their compelling narrative about simplifying online payments resonated with investors, leading to significant funding from venture capital firms like Sequoia Capital and Andreessen Horowitz.

Creating an impactful pitch deck is essential to capture investors' attention. Highlight the market opportunity, your team's expertise, the competitive landscape, and the financial projections. Showcase your technical capabilities and milestones achieved, such as successful product launches or partnerships.

When delivering your pitch, focus on presenting the problem, solution, and market opportunity with passion and conviction. Clearly articulate your vision, business model, and go-to-market strategy. Be prepared to answer investors' questions and address any concerns they may have. Demonstrating your ability to adapt and iterate based on user feedback and market dynamics can instill confidence in your startup's potential for success.

It's important to understand that investors not only invest in the product or service but also in the founding team. Highlight your technical skills, relevant experience, and your ability to execute. Surround yourself with a strong advisory board or mentors who can provide guidance and credibility.

Remember that each investor has their own investment thesis and preferences. Research potential investors and tailor your approach to align with their investment criteria and areas of interest. Building relationships with investors takes time, so be patient and persistent in your efforts.

Approaching investors as a developer-founder requires a strategic and well-prepared approach. By effectively showcasing your technical expertise, articulating market opportunities, and building compelling narratives, you can increase your chances of securing the funding and support needed to fuel your startup's growth.

Navigating the Fundraising Process

Understanding the Fundraising Process

Securing external funding involves a multi-stage process that requires careful navigation. Understanding the fundraising journey is essential for startup founders. The process typically begins with initial investor meetings, where founders have the opportunity to present their business ideas and showcase their potential. If there is mutual interest, further discussions and due diligence follow, allowing investors to thoroughly evaluate the startup's financials, market position, and growth potential.

Once both parties are aligned, term sheet negotiations commence. Term sheets outline the key terms and conditions of the investment, including valuation, equity ownership, and investor rights. This stage involves careful consideration and negotiation to ensure a fair and mutually beneficial agreement.

The final stage involves reaching a definitive agreement, which includes legal documentation and closing the investment. It is essential to involve legal counsel to ensure the terms are properly documented and protect the interests of both parties.

Throughout the fundraising process, managing investor relationships is crucial. Founders should focus on building trust, maintaining transparency, and providing regular updates to investors. Open and effective communication helps establish a strong rapport and fosters long-term partnerships.

Realizing the fundraising process can be demanding, but by understanding its stages and following best practices, founders can navigate the journey more effectively and increase their chances of securing the necessary funding for their startup's growth.

Fundraising Pitfalls and Lessons Learned

Fundraising can be a challenging process, and being aware of common pitfalls can help founders navigate it more effectively. One common pitfall is setting an unrealistic valuation for the startup. Overvaluing the company can deter potential investors and hinder the fundraising process. It is crucial for founders to conduct thorough market research, assess their startup's stage and traction realistically, and work with advisors to determine a fair and reasonable valuation.

Another important aspect is setting clear expectations with investors. Founders should communicate their business goals, growth plans, and timelines accurately. It is essential to be transparent about the potential risks and challenges the startup may face. This ensures that both parties have aligned expectations and can work together towards a shared vision.

Maintaining focus on business growth during the fundraising process is also crucial. It is easy to get caught up in the fundraising activities and lose sight of the core business. Founders should strike a balance between fundraising efforts and driving the growth of their startup. Demonstrating progress and achieving milestones during the fundraising process can significantly enhance the startup's attractiveness to investors.

By learning from the experiences of others and being mindful of these fundraising pitfalls, founders can approach the process with greater awareness and increase their chances of securing the funding they need to fuel their startup's growth.

Chapter 9
Product Launch and Growth Strategies

The success of a startup lies in its ability to effectively launch its product and drive sustainable growth. In this section, we will explore the strategies and techniques that can propel your product into the market and achieve rapid growth. We will delve into the concept of growth hacking, a mindset and set of techniques focused on rapid experimentation and iterative growth. We will discuss the power of data analytics in optimizing your product for continued success, providing insights into user behavior, product performance, and opportunities for improvement. By implementing these strategies and harnessing the power of data, you will be equipped to drive significant growth for your startup and establish a strong foundation for long-term success.

Launching Your Product to the Market

Understanding the Product Launch Process

A well-executed product launch is the cornerstone of a startup's success. We begin by emphasizing the importance of thoroughly understanding your target audience. By conducting extensive market research and customer analysis, you can gain invaluable insights into their needs, preferences, and pain points. For instance, when Apple launched the iPhone in 2007, they identified a gap in the market for a revolutionary mobile device that combined a phone, music player, and internet browser. This understanding allowed them to tailor their messaging and features to appeal to tech-savvy individuals seeking a single, versatile device.

Crafting compelling messaging is another crucial aspect of a successful product launch. By clearly communicating the value proposition of your product, you can capture the attention and interest of your target audience. For example, when Airbnb launched, they tapped into the desire for unique travel experiences by positioning themselves as a platform that allows users to book accommodations in local homes, creating a sense of belonging and authenticity.

Developing a comprehensive launch plan is essential for orchestrating a successful product launch. This involves setting clear objectives, defining key milestones, and creating a timeline for each stage of the launch. Slack, a popular team collaboration tool, executed a well-structured launch plan by initially targeting small tech startups and gradually expanding their user base. This approach allowed them to refine their product based on early adopter feedback before scaling to larger organizations.

Real-life examples of successful product launches provide invaluable insights into effective strategies and tactics. For instance, when Tesla launched the Model S, they orchestrated a meticulously planned event that showcased the car's groundbreaking features, generating widespread media coverage and building anticipation among potential buyers.

Building Buzz and Generating Excitement

A successful product launch goes beyond simply introducing your product to the market - it involves creating a buzz and generating excitement that captivates your target audience. Let's delve into the strategies and techniques that can help you build anticipation, generate interest, and create a sense of exclusivity and urgency around your product launch.

One powerful tool at your disposal is social media. By leveraging platforms such as Twitter, Facebook, Instagram, and LinkedIn, you can reach a wide audience and engage with potential customers directly. Consider sharing teasers, behind-the-scenes glimpses, and sneak peeks to pique curiosity and create a buzz around your upcoming launch. For example, when Apple introduced the Apple Watch, they utilized social media to tease the product, showcasing its design and features through captivating visuals and short video clips, which sparked excitement among their followers.

Pre-launch campaigns can also play a vital role in building anticipation and generating excitement. By offering early access or exclusive perks to a select group of individuals, you can create a sense of exclusivity and generate word-of-mouth buzz. Dropbox, a cloud storage platform, famously employed this strategy by providing early access to their product to attendees of a technology conference, which resulted in significant buzz and a rapid increase in sign-ups.

Collaborating with influencers and thought leaders in your industry can amplify your reach and lend credibility to your product. Identify influential individuals who align with your brand and have a substantial following, and consider partnering with them to promote your product. Their endorsement and positive reviews can create a ripple effect, generating excitement and trust among their followers. For instance, when GoPro launched their action cameras, they collaborated with professional athletes and adventurers who showcased the camera's capabilities in extreme and breathtaking situations, generating widespread excitement and interest.

Organizing events can be an effective way to create a memorable and impactful product launch. Whether it's a virtual webinar, a live demonstration, or an exclusive launch party, events provide an opportunity to showcase your product, interact with potential customers, and generate media coverage. Apple's product launch events have become legendary, with Steve Jobs delivering captivating presentations that not only introduced new products but also created a sense of anticipation and excitement among attendees and viewers worldwide.

By implementing these strategies and techniques, you can build anticipation, generate excitement, and create a buzz that sets the stage for a successful product launch.

Growth Hacking and User Acquisition

Techniques for Startups

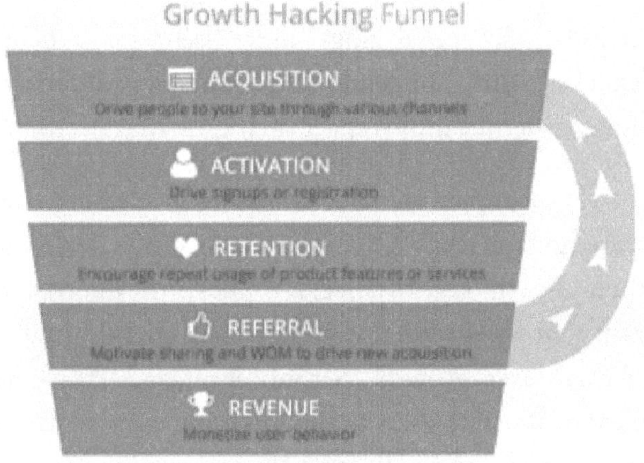

Understanding Growth Hacking

Growth hacking has emerged as a powerful approach that combines creativity, data analysis, and experimentation to drive exponential growth. At its core, growth hacking is a mindset that challenges traditional marketing approaches and embraces unconventional strategies to achieve growth. It involves leveraging data, technology, and creativity to identify high-impact growth opportunities and execute targeted experiments. While technical expertise is valuable in growth hacking, the focus is on adopting a growth-oriented mindset and employing innovative tactics to fuel startup growth.

To understand growth hacking, it's important to grasp the concept of the growth hacking funnel. The funnel consists of various stages, including user acquisition, activation, retention, revenue, and referral. Growth hackers focus on optimizing each stage of the funnel to drive user growth and maximize conversions. By analyzing user behavior, identifying bottlenecks, and implementing iterative improvements, startups can significantly impact their growth trajectory.

Real-world examples of successful growth hacking strategies showcase how startups have applied innovative techniques to fuel their growth. For instance, Dropbox introduced a referral program that incentivized users to invite friends, resulting in exponential user growth. Airbnb leveraged cross-platform integration, allowing users to sign up using their existing social media accounts, streamlining the onboarding process and increasing user acquisition. These examples highlight the power of creativity, data-driven decision-making, and strategic experimentation in achieving rapid growth.

User Acquisition Techniques for Startups

Acquiring users is a critical step towards achieving rapid growth. Startups can leverage various strategies to drive user acquisition and expand their customer base.

One powerful strategy for user acquisition is creating content tailored to the target audience. Startups can produce high-quality content, such as blog posts, tutorials, videos, or open-source projects, that addresses the needs and interests of their potential users. For example, a startup in the programming space can provide tutorials on the latest technologies or contribute to open-source projects, attracting developers who are seeking knowledge and insights.

Building and engaging with a targeted community can also be an effective user acquisition tactic. Startups can actively participate in online forums, discussion boards, and social media groups related to their product's niche. By providing valuable insights, support, and showcasing expertise, startups can establish relationships and gain visibility within their target audience. This organic approach often leads to word-of-mouth referrals and increased user acquisition.

Collaborating with other startups or companies that offer complementary products or services can be mutually beneficial for user acquisition. By forming partnerships, startups can access each other's user bases, cross-promote products, and share resources and expertise. These partnerships not only accelerate user acquisition but also create synergies that enhance the overall user experience.

Implementing referral programs is another powerful user acquisition technique. Startups can incentivize existing users to refer others to their platform by offering rewards or benefits. Referral programs tap into the power of word-of-mouth marketing, encouraging user engagement and expanding the startup's reach.

To optimize user acquisition efforts, it's essential to track and analyze relevant metrics. Startups can use tools like Google Analytics, Mixpanel, or Amplitude to monitor metrics such as conversion rates, user behavior, and acquisition channels. By analyzing this data, startups can make data-driven decisions to fine-tune their strategies and improve their user acquisition campaigns over time.

By employing these user acquisition techniques and embracing a growth hacking mindset, startups can drive significant growth and propel their businesses to success.

Leveraging Data Analytics for Product Optimization

The Power of Data Analytics

In the fast-paced world of startups, data analytics has emerged as a powerful tool for optimizing product performance and driving sustainable growth. To unlock the power of data analytics, it is crucial to establish a solid analytics infrastructure that captures relevant data points. Integration of tools such as Google Analytics, Mixpanel, or Amplitude into your product enables you to collect valuable insights on user behavior, engagement metrics, and conversion rates. By setting up the right analytics systems, startups can gain a comprehensive understanding of their product's performance.

Tracking key performance indicators (KPIs) is essential for evaluating the success of your product and identifying areas for improvement. User acquisition, retention rates, conversion funnels, and revenue generation are among the key metrics that startups should closely monitor. By tracking these KPIs, startups can make data-driven decisions and optimize user experience to drive growth.

Understanding user behavior is crucial for enhancing product performance. Techniques such as user segmentation, cohort analysis, and funnel analysis allow startups to gain insights into user interactions and identify patterns and bottlenecks. By conducting in-depth user behavior analysis, startups can uncover valuable insights that inform product iterations and enhancements.

A/B testing is a powerful technique for iteratively improving your product based on user feedback and data insights. By conducting controlled experiments and measuring statistically significant results, startups can iterate and optimize various aspects of their product. Real-world examples demonstrate how startups have utilized A/B testing to optimize user interfaces, features, and pricing strategies, leading to significant improvements and growth.

Real-world case studies highlight the transformative impact of data analytics on product performance and growth. These examples showcase how startups across different industries have leveraged data analytics to uncover actionable insights, make informed decisions, and achieve sustained growth. By embracing data analytics, startups can drive significant improvements in their product's performance, user experience, and overall success.

Continuous Improvement and Optimization

Continuous improvement and optimization are key drivers of success. By prioritizing user feedback loops, usability testing, and iterative development methodologies, startups can continually enhance their products and deliver exceptional user experiences.

In the pursuit of continuous improvement, startups need to foster a culture that values experimentation and learning from failures. Creating an environment where team members feel empowered to share ideas, take risks, and iterate on their work is crucial. By embracing this culture, startups can tap into the collective creativity and expertise of their team members to drive innovation.

User feedback is a valuable source of insights for optimizing products. By actively seeking and listening to user feedback through various channels, startups can gain a deep understanding of user needs and preferences. Usability testing plays a vital role in evaluating the effectiveness and user-friendliness of a product. By conducting tests with target users and analyzing their interactions, startups can gather valuable insights and identify areas for optimization.

Implementing iterative development methodologies like Agile and Lean enables startups to continuously refine their product based on user feedback, market changes, and emerging technologies. By embracing these methodologies, startups can stay agile, responsive, and proactive in meeting user needs and expectations.

****

Launching a product and achieving sustainable growth are key milestones in the startup journey. We explored the strategies and techniques necessary for a successful product launch. We delved into growth hacking and user acquisition techniques tailored for startups, emphasizing the importance of data analytics in optimizing your product for continued growth. By implementing these strategies and leveraging the power of data, you can maximize your product's potential and drive long-term success in the market.

The product launch process involves careful planning, coordination, and effective messaging to create excitement and generate interest among your target audience. Building buzz and anticipation through various channels, such as social media, pre-launch campaigns, and collaborations with influencers, can significantly impact the success of your launch.

Data analytics plays a crucial role in optimizing your product for sustained growth. By setting up robust analytics infrastructure, tracking key performance indicators (KPIs), conducting user behavior analysis, and leveraging A/B testing, you can make data-driven decisions and continuously improve your product.

Embracing a culture of continuous improvement and iteration is essential for long-term success. By actively seeking and incorporating user feedback, conducting usability testing, and implementing iterative development methodologies like Agile and Lean, you can refine your product based on user insights and market changes.

By effectively launching your product, leveraging growth hacking techniques, utilizing data analytics, and embracing continuous improvement, you can position your startup for rapid and sustainable growth.

Chapter 10
Incorporating Artificial Intelligence (AI)

Artificial Intelligence (AI) has emerged as a game-changer for startups, revolutionizing industries and opening up new possibilities. With its ability to analyze vast amounts of data, make predictions, and automate tasks, AI has become a powerful tool for driving innovation, enhancing efficiency, and delivering personalized experiences.

Machine learning, a subset of AI, plays a significant role in driving innovation. By harnessing the power of machine learning algorithms, startups can unlock valuable insights from their data and create intelligent, adaptive solutions.

Ethical considerations in AI development are paramount. By understanding AI's foundational concepts, identifying opportunities for integration, and considering ethical implications, startups can leverage AI to drive innovation, enhance competitiveness, and unlock new growth opportunities.

Understanding AI and Its Applications for Startups

Demystifying Artificial Intelligence

Artificial Intelligence (AI) is a rapidly evolving field that holds immense potential for startups. Machine learning, a prominent branch of AI, empowers systems to learn patterns and insights from data without explicit programming. Startups can leverage machine learning algorithms to automate tasks, personalize user experiences, and make data-driven predictions. For example, ride-sharing platforms like Uber use machine learning to optimize driver routes and predict surge pricing.

Natural Language Processing (NLP) is another facet of AI that focuses on enabling computers to understand and interact with human language. It finds application in virtual assistants like Siri and chatbots that facilitate customer support and enhance user engagement. Startups such as Grammarly, a writing assistance tool, utilize NLP to provide real-time grammar and spelling suggestions.

Computer vision, a field within AI, empowers machines to interpret and understand visual data. This technology enables startups to develop innovative applications such as facial recognition systems, object detection algorithms, and autonomous vehicles. For instance, the startup Zenuity utilizes computer vision to develop advanced driver-assistance systems (ADAS) for safer and more efficient driving experiences.

By understanding the core concepts of AI and its applications, startups can identify opportunities to integrate AI into their products and services. Real-world examples abound, from Netflix using AI-powered recommendation systems to optimize content suggestions, to Pinterest employing AI to improve image recognition and enhance user discovery.

AI Applications for Startups

AI offers a myriad of applications that can empower startups to differentiate themselves in the market.

Personalized Recommendations: Startups like Netflix and Spotify leverage AI algorithms to provide personalized content recommendations based on user preferences, viewing history, and behavior patterns. By analyzing vast amounts of data, they can offer tailored suggestions that enhance user engagement and satisfaction. For example, Netflix's recommendation engine uses machine learning algorithms to analyze user behavior and provide personalized movie and TV show recommendations, leading to increased user retention and customer loyalty.

Predictive Analytics: Companies like Blue Apron, a meal kit delivery service, use AI to analyze customer data and predict future meal preferences. By understanding individual tastes and dictary preferences, they can curate personalized meal plans and improve customer retention. Blue Apron's AI algorithms analyze customer feedback, ingredient preferences, and cooking history to suggest customized recipes, enhancing the overall dining experience and increasing customer satisfaction.

Intelligent Automation: Startups like UiPath offer AI-powered robotic process automation (RPA) solutions. These technologies automate repetitive tasks, such as data entry or invoice processing, freeing up employees to focus on higher-value work and increasing operational efficiency. By utilizing AI algorithms, UiPath's RPA platform can mimic human actions and automate business processes, leading to improved productivity and cost savings for organizations.

Chatbots: Many startups integrate AI-powered chatbots into their customer support systems. These chatbots can handle customer inquiries, provide instant responses, and offer personalized recommendations. Startups like Zendesk and Intercom utilize chatbots to enhance customer experiences and streamline support processes. For example, Intercom's AI-powered chatbot can engage in natural language conversations with customers, answer frequently asked questions, and escalate complex issues to human agents, ensuring efficient and personalized customer support.

These examples illustrate the diverse applications of AI in startups. By leveraging AI technologies, startups can deliver personalized experiences, optimize operations, and gain valuable insights from data.

Identifying Opportunities to Integrate AI

Assessing Your Startup's Needs and Challenges

Before incorporating AI into your startup, it's essential to assess your specific needs and challenges. By conducting a thorough assessment, you can determine the most suitable AI applications for your startup.

One key consideration is scalability. Startups often face challenges in scaling their operations to meet increasing demands. AI can help automate processes, optimize resource allocation, and handle large volumes of data, enabling your startup to scale efficiently and handle growth effectively.

Efficiency is another crucial aspect. AI technologies, such as machine learning algorithms, can streamline operations, automate repetitive tasks, and reduce manual effort. By leveraging AI-powered solutions, startups can improve operational efficiency, allowing their teams to focus on high-value activities.

Decision-making is another area where AI can make a significant impact. By analyzing large datasets and extracting valuable insights, AI can provide data-driven recommendations and support decision-making processes. Startups can leverage AI algorithms to gain actionable insights, identify trends, and make informed decisions that drive business growth.

Customer engagement is also a critical consideration. AI-powered chatbots, virtual assistants, and personalized recommendation systems can enhance customer experiences, provide instant support, and tailor offerings to individual preferences. By leveraging AI to deliver personalized and engaging experiences, startups can build strong customer relationships and foster loyalty.

By assessing your startup's needs and challenges, you can identify specific areas where AI can have the most significant impact. This understanding will guide you in selecting the right AI applications to integrate into your products or services.

Market Research and Industry Trends

Staying informed about market trends and industry developments is essential for identifying opportunities to integrate AI into your startup. By conducting thorough market research, you can gain insights into the latest advancements and trends in AI that are relevant to your industry.

Market research involves gathering information about your target market, competitors, and customer needs. It helps you understand the current landscape and identify areas where AI can provide unique value. By analyzing market trends, you can anticipate customer demands and align your AI integration strategy accordingly.

Additionally, staying updated on industry trends allows you to explore how other startups or established companies are leveraging AI in innovative ways. By studying successful case studies and real-life examples, you can gain inspiration and insights into potential AI applications for your own startup.

Industry events, conferences, and networking opportunities are valuable sources of information and provide platforms to connect with experts and thought leaders in the AI space. By attending these events and engaging in industry discussions, you can expand your knowledge and stay at the forefront of AI advancements.

Furthermore, exploring research papers, industry reports, and online resources specific to your industry can provide valuable insights into AI applications and emerging trends. Keeping an eye on academic research and collaborations can help you uncover cutting-edge AI techniques and methodologies.

By conducting thorough market research and staying updated on industry trends, you can identify gaps, challenges, and innovative opportunities where AI can make a significant impact. This knowledge will guide you in developing a strategic AI integration plan that aligns with your startup's goals and customer demands.

Leveraging Machine Learning and Data-Driven Insights

Machine Learning for Startups

Machine learning is a transformative technology that enables startups to leverage data and make intelligent decisions. By understanding the principles and techniques of machine learning, startups can unlock powerful capabilities to drive growth and innovation.

Supervised learning, one of the fundamental machine learning approaches, has been used by startups like Grammarly to develop intelligent writing assistants. Grammarly's machine learning models analyze text and provide suggestions for grammar, spelling, and style, helping users improve their writing skills.

On the other hand, unsupervised learning algorithms have been instrumental in startups like Airbnb. By applying clustering techniques to user behavior data, Airbnb can segment its users into different groups, enabling personalized recommendations and enhancing the user experience.

Feature engineering is another essential aspect of machine learning, where startups extract relevant features from raw data to enhance model performance. For instance, the startup Credit Karma utilizes feature engineering techniques to assess users' creditworthiness and provide personalized financial recommendations.

Model training and evaluation are critical stages in the machine learning pipeline. Startups like Netflix have excelled in this area, developing sophisticated recommendation algorithms that analyze user behavior and preferences to suggest personalized movie and TV show recommendations.

Overall, machine learning empowers startups to automate processes, make data-driven decisions, and optimize outcomes.

Whether it's improving customer experience, enhancing product recommendations, or streamlining operations, machine learning has proven to be a game-changer for startups in various industries.

Harnessing Data-Driven Insights

Data-driven insights are the cornerstone of successful AI implementation for startups. By harnessing the power of data, startups can gain valuable insights that drive informed decision-making and fuel innovation.

Data collection plays a crucial role in AI implementation. Startups like Spotify have leveraged user data to personalize music recommendations. By analyzing users' listening behavior and preferences, Spotify's recommendation system provides tailored playlists and recommendations, enhancing the user experience.

Ensuring data quality is equally important. Startups like Zappos, an online shoe retailer, have implemented quality control measures to ensure accurate product data. By cleansing and standardizing product information, Zappos improves search results and provides customers with relevant and reliable information.

Data preprocessing is another vital step in the data-driven AI pipeline. Startups like Stitch Fix, an online personal styling service, use data preprocessing techniques to analyze customer feedback and style preferences. By transforming and normalizing the data, Stitch Fix's algorithms can generate personalized clothing recommendations that align with each customer's unique style.

Data analysis and visualization are key techniques for extracting actionable insights. Startups like Fitbit utilize data analysis to track users' health and fitness data. By visualizing activity patterns and identifying trends, Fitbit helps users make informed decisions about their health and wellness.

Startups can harness the power of data-driven insights to gain a competitive edge. By collecting high-quality data, implementing effective preprocessing techniques, and leveraging data analysis and visualization, startups can unlock valuable insights that drive innovation, optimize their products or services, and deliver exceptional user experiences.

Chapter 11
Building a Strong Team

Building a strong team is a crucial aspect of establishing a successful startup. Attracting top talent is a critical step in building a strong team. We will discuss effective recruitment strategies, including leveraging online platforms, attending tech conferences, and cultivating relationships with universities and coding bootcamps. Additionally, we will explore the importance of defining clear job roles and responsibilities, as well as crafting compelling job descriptions that resonate with potential candidates.

Once you have assembled your team, fostering a culture of innovation and collaboration becomes paramount. We will explore strategies for creating an inclusive and supportive work environment, where team members feel empowered to share ideas, take ownership of their work, and collaborate effectively.

As your startup experiences growth and expansion, effectively scaling your technical team becomes a crucial consideration. We will explore strategies for managing team growth, such as implementing scalable hiring processes, cross-functional collaboration, and establishing effective communication channels.

By building a strong team, startups can leverage the collective skills and expertise of their members to drive innovation, overcome challenges, and achieve long-term success.

Hiring and Managing Developers in a Startup Environment

Defining Your Talent Requirements

Building a strong team begins with a clear understanding of the specific skill sets and expertise needed for your startup. To establish a solid technical team, you must identify the key roles and responsibilities that will be crucial to your startup's success. Whether it's software development, data analysis, UX design, or system administration, each role plays a vital part in shaping your product or service.

Crafting well-defined job descriptions is equally essential in the hiring process. A thoughtfully written job description outlines the responsibilities, qualifications, and expectations for each position, helping potential candidates grasp the scope of their potential role in your startup.

By having a clear vision of the skills and qualities you seek, you can efficiently identify individuals who align with your startup's mission and culture. These key talents will form the foundation of your team, propelling your startup towards its goals and fostering an environment of collaboration and innovation.

Sourcing and Attracting Top Talent

Finding and attracting top talent in a competitive market is a crucial challenge for startups building a strong technical team. Job boards like Indeed and LinkedIn have been valuable platforms for many startups to post their openings and connect with potential candidates. For example, a fast-growing AI startup used LinkedIn to highlight its cutting-edge projects, resulting in a significant increase in applications from experienced data scientists and machine learning engineers.

Social media platforms like Twitter and GitHub can also be powerful tools to engage with the developer community and promote job openings. A mobile app startup shared insights into their collaborative team environment on Twitter, attracting developers who resonated with their culture of innovation and teamwork.

Participating in networking events, such as hackathons and tech conferences, provides opportunities to connect with skilled professionals who are passionate about their craft. A fintech startup actively participated in developer conferences, where they not only showcased their product but also engaged with potential candidates who showed a keen interest in their domain.

Building a compelling employer brand is essential in attracting top talent. A software development startup crafted engaging blog posts and videos highlighting their team's diverse projects and work-life balance, leading to increased interest from developers who sought a dynamic and inclusive work environment.

Conducting Effective Interviews and Assessments

The interview and assessment process is a crucial step in identifying candidates who are the right fit for your startup's vision and culture. Technical interviews play a vital role in evaluating a candidate's coding skills and problem-solving abilities. Consider incorporating real-world scenarios and coding challenges relevant to your startup's projects. For example, a machine learning startup devised a coding test that involved building a recommendation system, enabling them to assess the candidate's technical expertise in their domain.

Assessing cultural fit is equally important to ensure the candidate aligns with your startup's values and collaborative spirit. Incorporate behavioral questions to gauge how candidates approach teamwork and handle challenges. A cybersecurity startup used behavioral questions to assess a candidate's response to ethical dilemmas, ensuring they align with the company's commitment to ethical practices.

Consider different interview formats, such as panel interviews or technical discussions with the team, to gain diverse perspectives on the candidate's skills and potential fit. For instance, a blockchain startup conducted a panel interview with both technical and non-technical team members to assess the candidate's communication and collaboration skills in cross-functional settings.

It is essential to maintain a fair and inclusive evaluation process to attract a diverse talent pool. Avoid bias in the interview process and provide equal opportunities for candidates of different backgrounds and experiences. A fintech startup implemented standardized interview rubrics to ensure a consistent and unbiased assessment of candidates.

By conducting interviews and assessments effectively, your startup can identify top talent that not only possesses the required technical skills but also aligns with your company's values and culture, fostering a strong and cohesive team that propels your startup's success.

Fostering a Culture of Innovation and Collaboration

Creating an Innovative Work Environment

An innovative work environment is fundamental to the success of startups. Encourage a culture that promotes risk-taking and experimentation. For instance, a software development startup implemented "Innovation Fridays," where team members were encouraged to work on passion projects or explore new technologies, leading to the creation of groundbreaking features for their product.

Emphasize open communication and idea-sharing platforms to facilitate collaboration among team members. A health tech startup used a virtual ideation board where employees could contribute ideas and provide feedback, leading to the development of new health-monitoring features.

Create regular feedback loops to provide team members with opportunities to share their insights and suggestions. A mobile app startup held weekly brainstorming sessions where developers and designers collaborated to solve challenges creatively and improve user experiences.

Celebrate and recognize innovative efforts to motivate and inspire your team. A gaming startup implemented "Innovation Awards" to honor outstanding contributions, encouraging employees to pursue innovative solutions and ideas.

By creating an innovative work environment that fosters creativity, encourages risk-taking, and values open communication, you empower your team to thrive and contribute their best to your startup's growth and success.

Cultivating Collaboration and Cross-Functional Teams

Collaboration and cross-functional teamwork are essential for driving innovation and achieving success in startups. Embrace agile methodologies that prioritize collaboration and communication. A fintech startup adopted Scrum, holding regular stand-up meetings to update team members on progress, challenges, and next steps. This approach improved transparency and facilitated continuous collaboration.

Utilize collaborative tools and platforms to enhance team communication and productivity. A SaaS startup implemented cloud-based project management tools, enabling real-time collaboration on tasks and fostering a sense of shared ownership among team members.

Create cross-functional teams that bring together diverse skill sets and expertise. A health and wellness startup formed cross-functional teams comprising developers, designers, and marketers. This approach accelerated product development and ensured a holistic approach to user experiences.

Break down silos between departments to encourage knowledge sharing and foster a collaborative culture. A travel tech startup organized regular "knowledge sharing sessions" where employees from different departments exchanged insights and innovative ideas.

By cultivating collaboration and promoting cross-functional teamwork, your startup can harness the collective creativity and expertise of its employees, leading to enhanced problem-solving capabilities and a more streamlined and efficient workflow.

Scaling Your Technical Team Effectively

Identifying Scalability Needs

As your startup gains momentum and experiences growth, it becomes crucial to identify when and how to scale your technical team effectively. Observe your current team's workload and capacity to recognize signs of strain and increased demand. If developers are consistently stretched thin, it might be an indication that additional resources are required.

Analyze your product roadmap and business projections to anticipate future growth and technical demands. If your startup is planning to launch new features or enter new markets, scaling the technical team may be necessary to meet those challenges.

Conduct regular performance reviews and gather feedback from your current team to understand their pain points and bottlenecks. Addressing these issues can help you optimize the team's productivity before scaling.

Consider the time taken to onboard new developers and integrate them into the team. If the onboarding process is becoming a bottleneck, it might be a sign that you need to hire in advance to maintain a smooth workflow.

Assess your startup's financial position and runway to determine the feasibility of expanding the technical team. Budget constraints and cash flow considerations should be factored into your scalability planning.

By proactively identifying scalability needs and understanding the demands of your growing startup, you can make informed decisions about expanding your technical team to support future growth effectively.

Onboarding and Retaining Talent

Effective onboarding is a critical aspect of integrating new team members into your startup's culture and workflows seamlessly. A well-designed onboarding process can significantly impact the success and productivity of new hires.

Start by developing a structured onboarding plan that includes clear objectives, timelines, and resources. Assign a mentor or buddy to guide new employees during their initial days, providing them with the necessary support and helping them navigate the startup's dynamics.

Introduce new hires to the team, ensuring they have the opportunity to interact with various members and understand their roles within the organization. Foster a welcoming and inclusive environment that encourages collaboration and knowledge-sharing.

Offer opportunities for continuous learning and professional development. Provide access to training resources, workshops, and conferences to help team members expand their skill sets and stay updated on the latest industry trends.

To retain top talent, focus on building a positive work environment that promotes work-life balance, recognition, and employee well-being. Offer competitive compensation packages and benefits to attract and retain high-performing developers.

Regularly conduct performance evaluations and provide constructive feedback to help team members grow and succeed. Recognize and reward exceptional contributions to reinforce a culture of excellence and motivation.

By investing in a well-structured onboarding process and creating a supportive and engaging work environment, you can foster long-term commitment and loyalty among your technical team members, contributing to the success and stability of your startup.

Chapter 12
Overcoming Technical Hurdles

The path of a startup is laden with technical challenges, and let's delve into these obstacles and provide actionable solutions to overcome them. From scaling your infrastructure to managing technical debt and ensuring high code quality, we explore practical strategies to tackle these hurdles and pave the way for sustained growth. By navigating these challenges effectively, your startup can build a strong technical foundation and stay agile in the fast-paced world of entrepreneurship.

Identifying and Understanding Key Challenges

Recognizing Common Technical Hurdles

Encountering technical hurdles is a natural part of the journey. As your startup grows and evolves, you are likely to face a variety of challenges that may impact your product's performance, scalability, and overall success. Recognizing and understanding these common technical obstacles is crucial to devise effective solutions and maintain a competitive edge.

One of the most prevalent challenges for startups is scalability limitations. As your user base expands, your infrastructure must be able to handle the increased load without sacrificing performance. Ensuring that your system can scale effortlessly to meet growing demands is essential for delivering a seamless user experience and sustaining growth.

Performance bottlenecks can also hinder the smooth functioning of your product. Identifying and addressing performance issues early on is vital to prevent user dissatisfaction and retain a competitive advantage.

Furthermore, integrating various systems and services can become intricate, particularly as your startup expands and adopts new technologies. Managing these complex integrations and ensuring seamless communication between different components is critical for maintaining operational efficiency.

Additionally, startups often rely on external services and APIs to enhance their products' functionalities. However, dependencies on external services can introduce vulnerabilities and potential points of failure. Ensuring robustness and contingency plans in such cases is necessary to maintain uninterrupted services.

By proactively recognizing these common technical hurdles, you can implement best practices and innovative solutions to overcome them. As a result, your startup can navigate through challenges more effectively, deliver a superior user experience, and achieve sustained growth in the competitive startup ecosystem.

Cultivating a Solution-Oriented Mindset

A solution-oriented mindset is a crucial asset for any startup founder or team member. As you face technical hurdles in the ever-evolving landscape of startups, adopting a proactive and resilient attitude towards challenges can make all the difference. This mindset empowers you to embrace problems as opportunities for growth and innovation.

When confronted with complex challenges, a solution-oriented approach involves breaking them down into smaller, manageable components. By deconstructing the problem, you gain a clearer understanding of its underlying issues, allowing you to address them systematically. This approach prevents you from feeling overwhelmed and encourages progress through achievable milestones.

Furthermore, fostering a solution-oriented mindset involves exploring various approaches and solutions. Instead of getting fixated on a single solution, remain open to experimenting with different ideas and strategies. By considering multiple perspectives, you increase your chances of finding the most effective and innovative solution.

In addition to technical skills, effective communication and collaboration play a pivotal role in developing a solution-oriented mindset. Encouraging open dialogue and idea-sharing among team members can lead to the emergence of novel solutions and approaches to challenges.

Moreover, learning from past experiences and failures is a fundamental aspect of a solution-oriented mindset. By reflecting on past hurdles and the strategies employed to overcome them, you gain valuable insights that can inform your future decision-making.

By embracing a solution-oriented mindset, you create a positive and empowering work environment that nurtures creativity, innovation, and growth. This mindset enables your startup to tackle technical hurdles head-on, paving the way for sustained success and continuous improvement in the dynamic world of startups.

Scaling Infrastructure to Meet Growing Demands

Recognizing the Need for Scalability

Scalability is a fundamental aspect of startup growth, ensuring that your technical infrastructure can accommodate increasing user demands and business expansion. As your startup gains traction and attracts a larger user base, it's crucial to recognize the signs that indicate the need for scaling your infrastructure.

One of the key indicators is increasing server load. As the number of users accessing your product or service grows, the load on your servers and databases increases as well. If your existing infrastructure struggles to handle this increased load, it can lead to performance issues and slow response times, negatively impacting the user experience.

Performance degradation is another telltale sign that your startup requires scalability. When your system experiences slowdowns or lags due to heavy user traffic, it's a clear signal that you need to upgrade your infrastructure to handle the growing demand efficiently.

Additionally, an inability to handle user demand can be a strong indication that scalability is necessary. If your startup experiences frequent crashes or outages during peak periods, it highlights the urgent need to scale your infrastructure to meet the demand and maintain a reliable service.

Recognizing the need for scalability is essential for planning ahead and ensuring your startup can handle future growth effectively. Implementing strategies such as horizontal and vertical scaling, load balancing, and cloud-based solutions can empower your startup with the capacity to adapt to increasing user demands while maintaining optimal performance and a seamless user experience. By proactively addressing scalability needs, your startup can position itself for sustained growth and success in the competitive market.

Strategies for Scaling Effectively

Scaling effectively is essential to support your startup's growth and provide a seamless user experience as demand increases. Evaluating cloud solutions is a crucial step in the scaling process. Cloud computing offers flexible and scalable resources that can be tailored to your startup's specific needs. By leveraging cloud services, you can dynamically allocate computing power and storage resources, ensuring your infrastructure can scale up or down based on demand. Cloud solutions also provide high availability and redundancy, minimizing the risk of downtime and ensuring consistent service delivery.

Optimizing resource allocation is another key aspect of effective scaling. By closely monitoring your system's performance and usage patterns, you can identify areas where resources are underutilized or overburdened. This knowledge enables you to allocate resources more efficiently, reducing wastage and maximizing the cost-effectiveness of your infrastructure.

Implementing efficient caching mechanisms is crucial for improving performance and reducing server load. Caching frequently accessed data or content helps minimize the need to retrieve information from databases or external sources repeatedly. This optimization can significantly improve response times and enhance the overall user experience.

Load balancing is a fundamental technique for distributing incoming traffic across multiple servers. By evenly distributing the workload, load balancing ensures that no single server becomes overloaded, enhancing system reliability and preventing performance bottlenecks.

Horizontal scaling is a powerful strategy that involves adding more servers or instances to your infrastructure as user demand grows. This approach allows your startup to handle increased traffic by spreading the load across multiple servers, ensuring each server remains at an optimal performance level.

By implementing these strategies and best practices, you can build a robust technical foundation that can accommodate growing user demands and ensure the scalability and reliability of your startup's infrastructure. Embracing these scalable solutions will enable your startup to thrive in a competitive market and position itself for sustainable growth and success.

Managing Technical Debt and Ensuring Code Quality

Understanding Technical Debt

In the fast-paced development cycles of startups, technical debt can accumulate as a consequence of expedited decisions and the need to deliver products quickly. Technical debt refers to the trade-offs made in the short term that may have long-term consequences on code maintainability, scalability, and overall product quality. It can manifest in various forms, such as code complexity, outdated dependencies, lack of automated tests, and suboptimal architectural choices.

For example, imagine Startup A, eager to meet market demands, rushes their product launch by taking shortcuts in the code to release new features quickly. As the product gains popularity and the user base grows, they encounter performance issues, frequent system failures, and difficulties in maintaining and extending their codebase. The technical debt they accumulated by neglecting code quality and best practices starts to impede their ability to deliver new features rapidly, and the product's overall stability suffers.

Recognizing the impact of technical debt on their product's stability and future development efforts, Startup A decides to prioritize addressing technical debt. They allocate dedicated development sprints to refactor and optimize critical parts of their codebase, update outdated libraries, and establish a comprehensive suite of automated tests. By doing so, they manage to reduce technical debt significantly, resulting in improved performance, enhanced maintainability, and an overall better user experience.

Addressing technical debt proactively is crucial for maintaining a robust and sustainable technical foundation. It involves careful consideration of the implications of shortcuts taken during development and setting aside time and resources to refactor and improve the codebase. By addressing technical debt early and consistently, startups can ensure the long-term viability of their products, reduce the risk of future challenges caused by technical debt, and foster a culture of code quality and innovation within their technical teams.

Prioritizing Code Quality and Refactoring

Maintaining high code quality is a foundational aspect of building a successful and sustainable startup. By adhering to coding standards, conducting regular code reviews, implementing automated testing, and fostering a culture of continuous improvement, startups can elevate their codebase to higher standards.

For instance, Startup B places a strong emphasis on code quality from the outset. They establish coding guidelines that outline best practices, code formatting standards, and naming conventions. As their development team grows, they conduct regular code reviews to ensure consistency and identify potential issues early on. Moreover, they implement an automated testing framework to assess code functionality and catch bugs before they reach the production environment.

In addition to maintaining code quality, periodic refactoring is essential to keep the codebase agile and adaptable. Startup B acknowledges the importance of addressing technical debt and schedules regular refactoring cycles. During these cycles, the team revisits existing code to make improvements, optimize performance, and eliminate redundancy. This proactive approach to refactoring helps them reduce technical debt, making it easier to introduce new features and maintain the codebase over time.

Prioritizing code quality and refactoring enables startups to produce reliable, maintainable, and scalable software. By investing in code quality and addressing technical debt proactively, startups can build a strong foundation for their technical team to innovate and drive the company's growth forward. Consistently refining the codebase fosters a culture of excellence and continuous improvement, positioning the startup for success in the ever-evolving tech landscape.

Chapter 13

Marketing and Branding: Elevating Your Startup's Visibility

A well-crafted marketing strategy that effectively communicates the value of your product or service is essential for the success of your startup. Understanding how branding influences consumers' decision-making processes will enable you to create a distinct brand identity that differentiates your startup from competitors and leaves a lasting impact on your audience. Defining your brand values and messaging will be explored as key elements in crafting an authentic and compelling brand identity that resonates with your target market.

By gaining insights into your target audience's mindset, preferences, and needs, you can create marketing campaigns that effectively engage and resonate with them. We will explore content marketing as a powerful tool to position your startup as a thought leader in the industry, providing valuable insights and solutions to address your audience's challenges.

Leveraging networks and connections within your industry will enable you to engage with potential customers and establish your startup as a valuable resource and trusted partner. By nurturing a vibrant community, your startup can foster loyalty, advocacy, and organic growth, amplifying your marketing efforts and driving sustainable success.

Effective marketing and branding are crucial for startups to thrive in today's competitive market. By crafting a compelling brand identity, implementing tailored marketing strategies, and building a strong community, your startup can elevate its visibility, establish credibility, and forge strong connections with its target audience, setting the stage for long-term growth and prosperity.

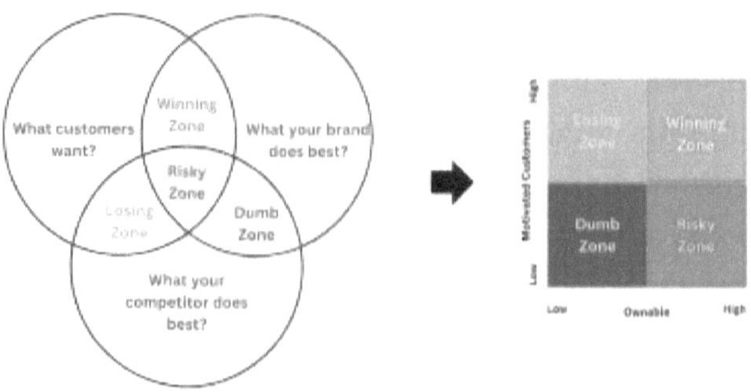

Crafting a Distinct Brand Identity

The Power of Branding

Branding emerges as a potent force that shapes how your company is perceived in the market. Beyond logos and visual aesthetics, branding encompasses the essence of your startup's identity and the emotions it evokes in your audience. A well-crafted and authentic brand identity can serve as a powerful differentiator, setting your product or service apart from competitors and leaving a lasting impression on consumers.

Understanding the profound impact of branding on consumers' decision-making processes is essential for startups seeking to gain a competitive edge. A compelling brand identity not only captures attention but also builds trust and credibility with your target audience. By aligning your startup's values, mission, and unique selling proposition with your branding efforts, you can create a strong emotional connection with consumers, fostering loyalty and advocacy.

Branding allows your startup to craft a narrative that communicates the essence of your offering and the benefits it brings to customers. It goes beyond the functional aspects of your product or service, delving into the realm of emotions and aspirations. A well-defined brand identity can evoke specific feelings, evoke memories, and ultimately influence purchasing decisions.

As a startup founder, recognizing the power of branding is a critical step towards establishing a strong foothold in the market. By investing time and effort into crafting an authentic and compelling brand identity, you can position your startup for success, effectively communicate its value proposition, and forge lasting relationships with your target market.

Defining Your Brand Values and Messaging

At the heart of a compelling brand identity lies a clear definition of your startup's core values and a powerful messaging strategy. Defining your brand values involves articulating the principles and beliefs that guide your company's decisions, actions, and interactions. These values serve as the foundation upon which your startup's identity is built and create a sense of purpose that resonates with your audience.

Crafting authentic messaging is equally essential to effectively communicate your startup's mission and unique value proposition. Your messaging should be consistent, transparent, and relatable, reflecting the aspirations and needs of your target audience. By conveying your startup's story in a genuine and compelling manner, you can establish an emotional connection with your audience, fostering trust and loyalty.

Defining your brand values and messaging requires a deep understanding of your startup's identity, vision, and target market. It involves conducting thorough market research to identify your audience's pain points, preferences, and motivations. By aligning your messaging with your audience's needs, you can ensure that your brand resonates with them on a personal level.

Moreover, incorporating your brand values into every aspect of your startup's operations, from product development to customer service, reinforces your commitment to authenticity and consistency. This alignment across all touchpoints creates a cohesive brand experience and strengthens your startup's position in the market.

By establishing a strong emotional connection with your audience through your brand identity, you can lay the groundwork for a successful marketing campaign that engages, inspires, and drives sustainable growth for your startup.

Customer-Focused Marketing Strategies

Understanding Your Target Audience

A successful marketing strategy begins with a thorough understanding of your target audience. By gaining insights into their needs, preferences, and pain points, you can craft campaigns that resonate with them on a personal level. Conducting comprehensive market research and customer analysis is essential to gather the data needed to make informed decisions and tailor your approach.

Market research involves analyzing industry trends, competitor activities, and customer behavior to identify opportunities and potential challenges. Understanding the competitive landscape enables you to position your startup uniquely and differentiate your product or service from others in the market.

Customer analysis delves deeper into the characteristics and behaviors of your existing customers and potential leads. By conducting surveys, interviews, and analyzing data, you can identify patterns, preferences, and pain points that drive your target audience's decision-making processes.

By understanding your target audience, you can segment them into distinct groups based on their demographics, behaviors, and interests. This segmentation allows you to create personalized marketing campaigns that speak directly to the specific needs and aspirations of each group.

Furthermore, understanding your target audience enables you to choose the most appropriate marketing channels and communication strategies. Whether it's social media, content marketing, email campaigns, or influencer marketing, knowing where and how to reach your audience effectively maximizes the impact of your efforts.

By investing time and resources into gaining insights, you can build a solid foundation for your marketing strategies, ensuring that your startup's messages and offerings resonate with the right people at the right time.

Content Marketing and Thought Leadership

Content marketing is an integral part of any successful marketing strategy. By creating valuable and relevant content, you can engage your audience and position your startup as a thought leader in your industry.

The key to effective content marketing lies in understanding your audience's needs and aspirations. By conducting thorough research and customer analysis, you can identify the topics, pain points, and interests that matter most to your customers. Armed with this knowledge, you can create content that addresses their challenges and provides practical solutions.

Blog posts are an excellent platform for sharing in-depth insights, tips, and best practices. By crafting compelling and informative blog posts, you can establish your startup as an authority in your field and build trust with your audience.

Informative articles and whitepapers allow you to delve into complex topics and provide valuable knowledge to your customers. By offering in-depth analysis and research, you can position your startup as a reliable source of information.

Social media content plays a crucial role in engaging your audience and fostering a community around your brand. By sharing bite-sized content, such as infographics, videos, and quotes, you can spark conversations and increase brand awareness.

Thought leadership content showcases your startup's expertise and innovation. By sharing your unique insights and perspectives on industry trends and emerging technologies, you can establish your startup as a forward-thinking leader in your field.

Content marketing goes beyond just creating content; it also involves distributing and promoting it effectively. By leveraging various channels such as social media, email marketing, and influencer collaborations, you can reach a wider audience and amplify the impact of your content.

Building a Vibrant Community

Leveraging Online Networks

Building a strong and engaged community is a powerful way to foster loyalty, advocacy, and organic growth for your startup. Social media platforms offer a dynamic space for connecting with your audience and showcasing your startup's personality. By sharing relevant content, responding to comments and messages, and actively participating in discussions, you can build meaningful relationships with your followers and strengthen your brand presence.

Forums and discussion boards are valuable channels for engaging with your target audience and industry peers. By actively participating in these communities and offering valuable insights and expertise, you can establish your startup as a thought leader and trusted authority in your field.

Industry-specific communities and groups provide targeted spaces for connecting with your niche audience. By joining these communities and contributing valuable content and discussions, you can build credibility and forge strong connections with potential customers and partners.

Engagement is key to nurturing your online community. Responding promptly to inquiries, addressing feedback, and showing appreciation for your community's support cultivates a positive and welcoming environment.

Establishing your startup as a valuable resource and trusted partner involves offering meaningful support and solutions to your community. By providing valuable resources, hosting webinars or workshops, and offering exclusive benefits to your community members, you can foster a sense of belonging and loyalty.

By building and nurturing a vibrant community around your startup, you can create a loyal and engaged customer base, amplify your brand's reach, and drive sustainable growth for your startup in the competitive market.

Nurturing Customer Engagement

Building strong and lasting relationships with your customers is a cornerstone of successful marketing. Webinars and interactive events provide valuable opportunities for direct engagement with your customers. By hosting informative webinars and interactive events, you can offer insights, answer questions, and gather feedback in real-time. These interactions not only strengthen your brand's authority but also foster a sense of community among your customers.

User-generated content (UGC) campaigns are a powerful way to involve your customers in your marketing efforts. Encouraging customers to create and share content related to your brand or products not only boosts engagement but also serves as authentic social proof for your startup. UGC campaigns can range from customer testimonials and product reviews to creative content such as photos, videos, or blog posts.

Personalization is key to connecting with your customers on a deeper level. Tailoring your communications and content to individual preferences and interests can significantly enhance engagement. Use data-driven insights to segment your audience and deliver personalized messages, recommendations, and offers.

Loyalty programs and exclusive benefits can incentivize repeat purchases and advocacy. By rewarding loyal customers with special offers, discounts, or access to exclusive content or events, you reinforce the value they receive from your brand and encourage continued engagement.

Feedback and customer support are essential components of customer engagement. Actively listening to your customers' feedback, addressing their concerns promptly, and providing exceptional customer support build trust and demonstrate your commitment to customer satisfaction. By putting your customers at the center of your marketing efforts and fostering meaningful interactions, you can create a loyal customer base, amplify your brand's reach, and drive sustained growth for your startup in the competitive market.

Chapter 14

Lessons from Successful Startup Founders: Insights and Inspiration for Developer-Founders

The experiences and journeys of successful founders hold invaluable lessons and inspiration. Whether you are an aspiring developer-founder or an entrepreneur seeking inspiration for your own venture, this book presents a treasure trove of wisdom and guidance to help you navigate the exciting and often unpredictable world of entrepreneurship.

The Founders' Journeys

From Developer to Founder: Embracing the Entrepreneurial Path

The stories of successful founder-developers serve as beacons of inspiration and valuable sources of wisdom. From the spark of an idea to the audacious decision to take the plunge, we explore the challenges they faced, the risks they took, and the rewards they reaped.

The Genesis of Entrepreneurial Dreams

Meet Jane, a seasoned software developer with a passion for creating innovative solutions. For years, Jane had honed her technical skills while working for various tech companies. However, she always felt a deep desire to do more, to create something that would make a meaningful impact on people's lives. The turning point came during a personal experience when she struggled to find meaningful volunteering opportunities in her community. This ignited her desire to create a platform that made it easier for people to give back and connect with local nonprofit organizations. And thus, the seed of her startup was planted.

Similarly, we encounter Alex, a talented developer with a heart for sustainability. The fast fashion industry's environmental impact deeply concerned him, and he envisioned a world where consumers could make sustainable shopping choices with ease. Driven by his passion for sustainability, Alex embarked on a journey to found a startup that utilized AI and data analytics to empower conscious consumers. His vision was to create a positive impact on the environment by encouraging sustainable consumer behavior.

Overcoming Obstacles and Taking Risks

For both Jane and Alex, the journey from developer to founder was marked by moments of uncertainty and courage. Turning their ideas into reality meant taking significant risks and navigating uncharted territory. Funding their startups was a major challenge. Jane sought investors who shared her vision for creating a volunteering platform that fostered community engagement and social impact. With resilience and determination, she secured seed funding that enabled her to kickstart the development of her app.

Alex faced similar hurdles as he sought funding to fuel the growth of his sustainable fashion startup. Pitching his idea to investors was a nerve-wracking experience, but his passion and dedication to his vision shone through. It was a leap of faith, but he secured the necessary funding to take his startup to the next level.

Assembling the Right Pieces

The success of any startup hinges on a strong and diverse team. For Jane and Alex, assembling a team that shared their vision and brought complementary skills to the table was paramount. Jane knew that to create a user-friendly and impactful volunteering platform, she needed a team that combined technical expertise with a deep understanding of community needs. Together, they worked tirelessly to develop a platform that connected volunteers with local nonprofits seamlessly.

Similarly, Alex recognized the significance of a team that shared his passion for sustainability and possessed the technical prowess to develop an innovative platform. Together, they brought to life an AI-powered solution that provided consumers with transparent information on the sustainability of clothing brands.

Perseverance and Adaptability

Entrepreneurship is a rollercoaster ride of highs and lows, and Jane and Alex experienced their fair share of challenges and setbacks. Technical hurdles, unforeseen market shifts, and fierce competition tested their resolve. But through it all, their determination and adaptability prevailed.

Jane's platform encountered technical challenges that required constant iteration and improvements. As she navigated the startup landscape, she learned to embrace failure as an opportunity for growth. The setbacks became learning experiences, and the platform evolved into a powerful tool for social impact.

For Alex, staying ahead in the fast-paced world of sustainable fashion technology demanded constant adaptation. The market dynamics were ever-changing, and he had to pivot the platform's features to cater to evolving consumer needs. The ability to adapt and learn from failures was crucial in maintaining the startup's relevance and market position.

The Rewards of Purpose-Driven Entrepreneurship

The rewards of entrepreneurship extended far beyond financial success for Jane and Alex. For Jane, seeing her platform connecting thousands of volunteers with local nonprofits brought immense satisfaction. She witnessed the impact of her startup on communities, and the heartfelt testimonials from volunteers and nonprofits filled her with pride.

Alex experienced the fulfillment of knowing that his platform had empowered thousands of consumers to make sustainable choices. As more people adopted sustainable shopping habits, he saw the positive impact on the environment unfold before his eyes.

Lessons from Visionary Developer-Founders

The experiences of Jane and Alex offer a wealth of knowledge and inspiration for aspiring developer-founders. Their stories demonstrate the power of innovation, the impact of unwavering determination, and the rewards of pursuing a vision with passion and purpose. As you embark on your own entrepreneurial journey, remember that success lies not only in technical prowess but in the courage to dream big, the resilience to overcome challenges, and the determination to create a positive change in the world.

Through the triumphs and challenges of Jane and Alex, we gain valuable insights into the transformative journey of entrepreneurship. Their stories serve as a testament to the transformative power of entrepreneurship, where challenges become opportunities and perseverance paves the way for success. As you navigate the exciting and often unpredictable world of startups, may the lessons and experiences of these visionary developer-founders guide you towards your own path of success and fulfillment.

Navigating the Startup Landscape: Overcoming Challenges and Seizing Opportunities

The path of an entrepreneur is riddled with challenges and opportunities, and founder-developers like Jane and Alex had their fair share of hurdles to overcome. As they embarked on their startup journeys, they encountered a myriad of obstacles that tested their resolve and ingenuity.

For Jane, building a volunteering platform that catered to both volunteers and nonprofits was no easy feat. Technical challenges arose as the team worked to develop a seamless user experience while ensuring data security and privacy. The complexities of integrating various systems and APIs demanded innovative solutions and long hours of problem-solving. However, Jane and her team tackled each obstacle with unwavering determination, seeking guidance from mentors and learning from industry experts to find the best solutions.

Alex faced a different set of challenges in the competitive world of sustainable fashion. As his platform gained traction, he encountered increased competition from larger players in the market. Maintaining a competitive edge required constant innovation and adaptability. Alex embraced these challenges as opportunities to redefine his platform's unique selling points and differentiate it from competitors. He actively sought feedback from early adopters to improve the user experience and refine his platform's value proposition.

Fundraising was another critical aspect of their startup journeys. Jane and Alex recognized that securing funding was vital to fuel their growth and expand their impact. However, convincing investors to believe in their vision was no easy task. They honed their pitch, showcasing the social impact of their startups and the potential for scalable growth. With perseverance and a compelling story, they successfully attracted investors who shared their passion for creating positive change.

Despite the challenges, Jane and Alex also seized numerous opportunities that presented themselves along the way. Networking events, industry conferences, and community gatherings provided invaluable connections and insights. They actively engaged with potential partners and collaborators, leveraging these relationships to expand their reach and enhance their offerings.

Throughout their journeys, both Jane and Alex recognized the significance of adaptability and resilience. Market shifts and changing consumer demands required them to pivot their strategies and offerings. Rather than viewing these shifts as setbacks, they embraced them as opportunities to learn and evolve. By remaining agile and open to feedback, they navigated the ever-changing startup landscape with confidence.

As their startups gained momentum, Jane and Alex also understood the importance of prioritizing their team's well-being and fostering a positive work culture. They recognized that a motivated and engaged team was crucial to overcoming challenges and driving innovation. Through team-building activities, clear communication, and continuous learning opportunities, they cultivated a supportive environment that encouraged their team to thrive.

The journeys of Jane and Alex exemplify the transformative power of entrepreneurship. As they turned their visions into reality, they demonstrated the importance of tenacity, innovation, and adaptability in navigating the startup landscape. Their experiences serve as valuable lessons for aspiring developer-founders, offering guidance on overcoming challenges and seizing opportunities with resilience and ingenuity.

Insights and Lessons Learned

Vision, Strategy, and Execution: Building a Solid Foundation for Success

The journey of successful startup founders is marked by their unwavering vision, strategic acumen, and meticulous execution. As they embarked on their entrepreneurial quests, they laid a solid foundation for their startups by honing their vision, crafting a clear strategy, and meticulously executing their plans.

For Sarah, the founder of a health tech startup, defining a compelling vision was the first step towards success. Inspired by her personal experience with a health condition, Sarah envisioned a world where healthcare was accessible and personalized for everyone. Her vision centered around leveraging technology to empower patients and healthcare providers alike. With a clear sense of purpose, Sarah set out to develop a platform that revolutionized the healthcare experience.

Similarly, John, the founder of an AI-driven e-commerce platform, understood the significance of a strong strategic direction. He envisioned a marketplace that seamlessly connected buyers and sellers, revolutionizing the way people shopped online. John meticulously analyzed market trends, identified gaps, and crafted a strategy that positioned his platform as a disruptive force in the e-commerce space.

As their visions took shape, these founders turned their attention to execution. Building a startup requires a fine balance between planning and adaptability. Sarah focused on achieving product-market fit by continuously gathering feedback from users and iterating on her platform's features. She emphasized the importance of listening to her customers and incorporating their needs into her product's roadmap.

John, on the other hand, implemented a scalable growth strategy for his e-commerce platform. He leveraged data analytics and AI algorithms to optimize user experiences, personalized recommendations, and efficient inventory management. As his platform gained traction, he navigated scaling challenges by strategically expanding his team and infrastructure.

Team building emerged as a critical aspect of execution for both founders. Sarah and John understood that their teams were instrumental in bringing their visions to life. They prioritized hiring individuals who shared their passion for the startup's mission and aligned with their values. Creating a positive work culture and fostering an environment of collaboration and innovation enabled their teams to perform at their best.

Throughout their journeys, Sarah and John also emphasized the importance of staying customer-centric. They recognized that customer feedback was invaluable in refining their products and services. By actively engaging with their users, they gained insights that allowed them to deliver solutions that precisely met their customers' needs.

As Sarah and John navigated the unpredictable waters of entrepreneurship, they learned to embrace uncertainty and adapt to changing market dynamics. They emphasized the importance of being agile and resilient, iteratively improving their strategies based on real-world data and insights.

The experiences of Sarah and John exemplify the trifecta of success in the startup world: vision, strategy, and execution. By starting with a compelling vision, defining a clear strategic direction, and executing their plans with precision, they laid a solid foundation for their startups. Their journeys teach us the importance of adapting to challenges, staying customer-centric, and building strong teams to navigate the dynamic entrepreneurial landscape.

As you embark on your own startup journey, remember that a strong vision serves as a guiding light, a clear strategy keeps you on track, and meticulous execution turns dreams into reality. Embrace the lessons learned from visionary founders like Sarah and John, and approach your startup with determination, resilience, and a relentless focus on delivering value to your customers.

Embracing Failure and Learning from Setbacks

The path of entrepreneurship is fraught with challenges and setbacks, and every founder faces moments of failure.

For Emily, the founder of a social media analytics startup, failure became a transformative experience. Early in her journey, her product launch didn't generate the expected traction, and user feedback highlighted areas that needed improvement. Rather than letting this setback deter her, Emily saw it as a chance to iterate and enhance her product. She sought feedback from users, conducted in-depth market research, and collaborated with her team to make the necessary enhancements. Emily's resilience and adaptability not only led to a significantly improved product but also helped her build a stronger connection with her user base.

Similarly, David, the founder of a fintech platform, faced challenges when seeking funding from investors. Rejections were disheartening, but David reframed these experiences as learning opportunities. He analyzed the feedback received, identified areas for improvement in his pitch, and worked diligently to address investors' concerns. Through perseverance and continuous refinement, David honed his pitch, ultimately securing funding from an investor who saw the potential in his startup. This experience taught David the value of persistence and the importance of learning from failures to move closer to success.

Throughout their journeys, both Emily and David maintained a growth mindset, seeing each setback as an opportunity to learn, improve, and evolve. They recognized that setbacks were not indicators of failure but rather stepping stones on the path to success. By embracing failure and reframing setbacks as learning experiences, they nurtured a culture of resilience within their teams and fostered an environment where experimentation and innovation thrived.

As founder-entrepreneurs, Emily and David demonstrated the importance of maintaining self-belief and not allowing failure to define them. They persevered through adversity, drawing upon their experiences to propel their startups forward. Their stories serve as a reminder that setbacks are an inherent part of the entrepreneurial journey, and by embracing failure, one can transform challenges into opportunities for growth and improvement.

The entrepreneurial spirit is defined not just by successes but also by how founders navigate failures and setbacks. Emily and David's experiences exemplify the resilience and determination that fuel visionary founders to overcome challenges. By seeing failures as stepping stones to success and learning from setbacks, they demonstrated the true essence of entrepreneurship.

As you embark on your own startup journey, remember that setbacks are inevitable but can be transformative. Embrace failure with a growth mindset, learn from your experiences, and use them to propel your startup forward. The road to success may be riddled with challenges, but it is also paved with invaluable lessons and opportunities for growth. By embracing failure, you can unleash the full potential of your entrepreneurial spirit and set yourself on a path to success in the dynamic world of startups.

Advice and Inspiration for Developer-Founders

Key Lessons and Nuggets of Wisdom

The stories of these successful founder-entrepreneurs offer a treasure trove of valuable insights and lessons for aspiring developer-founders. Their experiences have shaped their understanding of the startup landscape, and in this section, we present a compilation of key lessons and nuggets of wisdom they have to offer.

Lesson 1: Resilience in the Face of Adversity

Every founder-entrepreneur faces challenges, but what sets them apart is their resilience. These visionary leaders emphasized the importance of staying resilient in the face of adversity. Whether it was overcoming technical hurdles, facing market competition, or navigating the uncertainties of fundraising, they advised never to lose sight of the bigger picture and to maintain unwavering determination.

Lesson 2: Embracing Innovation and Continuous Learning

Innovation lies at the heart of successful startups. The founder-entrepreneurs stressed the significance of embracing innovation and continuously learning from both successes and failures. They encouraged aspiring founders to remain open to new ideas, stay curious, and be willing to pivot when necessary to stay ahead in a rapidly evolving market.

Lesson 3: Building and Nurturing a Strong Team

The success of any startup hinges on the strength of its team. These founders emphasized the importance of building a cohesive and high-performing team. They advised aspiring founders to focus on hiring for cultural fit and values alignment, rather than just technical skills. Nurturing a strong team culture built on trust, collaboration, and open communication was also highlighted as essential for long-term success.

Lesson 4: Developing a Clear Vision and Strategic Focus

A clear vision and strategic focus are essential guiding principles for startups. The founder-entrepreneurs stressed the importance of defining a compelling vision for their startups and aligning all efforts toward achieving that vision. Having a well-defined strategy allowed them to make informed decisions and prioritize their efforts effectively.

Lesson 5: Maintaining a Customer-Centric Approach

In the dynamic world of startups, customers are the heartbeat of success. These founders emphasized the value of a customer-centric approach, which involves actively listening to customers' feedback, understanding their needs, and incorporating their insights into product development and improvement. They stressed that a deep understanding of customer pain points is instrumental in crafting products that truly resonate with the target audience.

Lesson 6: Networking and Building Relationships

Networking and building meaningful relationships play a crucial role in the growth of startups. The founder-entrepreneurs advised aspiring founders to actively participate in industry events, conferences, and developer communities to expand their network and gain valuable insights from peers and mentors. These relationships often open doors to new opportunities and collaborations.

Lesson 7: Balancing Pragmatism and Ambition

Startups walk a fine line between pragmatism and ambition. The founder-entrepreneurs acknowledged the importance of setting ambitious goals while remaining pragmatic in execution. Being agile and adaptable to changing circumstances was seen as a key attribute in the pursuit of long-term success.

The collective wisdom of these founder-entrepreneurs serves as a roadmap for aspiring developer-founders to navigate the exciting and unpredictable world of startups. Their lessons on resilience, innovation, team building, strategic focus, customer-centricity, networking, and balancing pragmatism and ambition offer invaluable guidance for building a successful startup.

As you embark on your own entrepreneurial journey, remember that each challenge presents an opportunity for growth and learning. Embrace the entrepreneurial spirit, stay curious, and remain resilient in the face of adversity. By incorporating these key lessons into your startup's foundation, you can pave the way for a rewarding and impactful journey as a developer-founder in the dynamic world of startups.

Inspiration and Motivation

The stories of these founder-entrepreneurs go beyond the technical and business aspects of building a startup. Through their stories and experiences, you will discover the passion, dedication, and entrepreneurial spirit that fuel their journey.

Passion as the Driving Force: Each founder-entrepreneur is fueled by an unyielding passion for their vision. Their startups are not merely businesses; they are extensions of their deepest beliefs and desires to make a meaningful impact. Their passion for their products and services shines through, motivating them to overcome challenges and persevere even in the face of uncertainty.

The Impact Motive: For these visionaries, the desire to create a positive impact on the world is a powerful motivator. They are driven by the belief that their startups can make a difference in people's lives, whether by solving a pressing problem, enhancing efficiency, or enriching experiences. This sense of purpose fuels their determination and keeps them focused on their mission.

The Thrill of Innovation: Innovation is at the heart of every startup, and these founder-entrepreneurs are no exception. The thrill of exploring new ideas, pushing boundaries, and disrupting traditional norms energizes them on their journey. They embrace the challenges that come with innovation and see each obstacle as an opportunity to create something extraordinary.

Learning and Growth: The journey of building a startup is a continuous process of learning and growth. These founders have a voracious appetite for knowledge and constantly seek opportunities to expand their horizons. They view setbacks as learning experiences and use failures as stepping stones toward improvement. This hunger for growth fuels their resilience and adaptability.

Inspiration from Role Models: Behind every founder-entrepreneur, there are role models and mentors who have inspired them along the way. Whether it's a renowned entrepreneur, a leader in their industry, or a family member, these role models serve as beacons of inspiration, guiding them through challenges and providing encouragement during difficult times.

The Impact of a Supportive Community: Building a startup is not a solitary journey. These founder-entrepreneurs emphasize the importance of a supportive community that includes family, friends, team members, and fellow entrepreneurs. The encouragement, feedback, and camaraderie within their communities contribute significantly to their motivation and sense of belonging.

A Legacy to Leave Behind: Beyond the immediate success of their startups, these founders are driven by the desire to create a lasting legacy. They envision their startups as a testament to their hard work, dedication, and vision. Leaving behind a legacy that inspires future generations of entrepreneurs motivates them to persist and build something greater than themselves.

Embarking on Your Journey with Purpose

The personal philosophies, motivations, and sources of inspiration that drive these founder-entrepreneurs serve as a source of motivation and inspiration for aspiring developer-founders. As you embark on your own entrepreneurial journey, remember that passion, purpose, innovation, learning, and a supportive community are the pillars that will propel you forward. Stay inspired, remain true to your vision, and embrace the challenges with unwavering determination. The world of startups offers immense potential and possibilities, and through your journey, you too can make a profound impact and leave a lasting legacy.

The Startup CodeBook

In closing, "The Startup Codebook: From Developer to Entrepreneur" has been an incredible journey through the dynamic world of startups and the transformative power of entrepreneurial pursuits. We've explored the captivating intersection of coding skills and the entrepreneurial mindset, witnessing how developers can evolve into successful founder-entrepreneurs.

Throughout these pages, we've dived into the essential elements of building a startup, from ideation and validation to choosing the right tech stack and developing a minimum viable product. We've uncovered the significance of leveraging cloud technologies, navigating funding strategies, and embracing artificial intelligence to drive innovation.

The challenges of scaling technical infrastructure, overcoming technical hurdles, and fostering a strong team culture have been met with strategic solutions and valuable insights. Moreover, we've unraveled the vital importance of marketing and branding in elevating a startup's visibility and building a passionate community around its product or service.

Through real-life examples, interviews, and case studies of inspiring developer-founders, we've been gifted with the wisdom and guidance needed to navigate the unpredictable landscape of entrepreneurship. Their experiences, both triumphs, and setbacks, serve as beacons of light, reminding us that resilience, determination, and an unwavering belief in our vision can lead to remarkable success.

As you embark on your own entrepreneurial journey, remember that this book is merely the beginning. Embrace the challenges, embrace the failures, and embrace the growth. Your path will undoubtedly be unique, but know that the lessons shared here and the knowledge gained will serve as your faithful companions.

In the ever-evolving landscape of startups, continue to seek knowledge, adapt, and innovate. Your passion and dedication, combined with the technical expertise honed through countless coding hours, will forge a path toward creating something extraordinary.

From ideation to validation, from building a strong team to overcoming technical hurdles, remember that each step is a building block, shaping the foundation of your startup's success. Stay true to your vision, embrace the entrepreneurial spirit within you, and let your passion drive you forward.

As I conclude this book, I extend my heartfelt gratitude to all the inspiring developer-founders, industry experts, and entrepreneurs who have shared their invaluable wisdom and experiences. Their stories have enriched these pages, leaving us with a treasure trove of insights to draw from.

I wish you the utmost success in your startup endeavors. Remember, the journey may be arduous at times, but with determination, innovation, and a never-ending thirst for learning, you will create something remarkable and change the world in your own unique way.

Dream big, code passionately, and let your entrepreneurial spirit soar.

With warm regards,

Anish Bilas Panta

Author of "The Startup Codebook: From Developer to Entrepreneur"

About The Author

Anish Bilas Panta

Meet Anish Bilas Panta, a seasoned software architect and solution provider with a passion for empowering businesses through cutting-edge technology. As the author of "The Startup Codebook: From Developer to Entrepreneur," Anish brings over 10 years of experience in the industry, making him a reliable guide for aspiring developer-founders.

Anish's journey has been shaped by valuable lessons learned from the failures of multiple startups and his experience in joining startups from their early phases. With expertise in FinTech and InsurTech industries, he has been an integral part of building businesses from scratch, contributing to their growth and success.

Not only an accomplished developer, but Anish also possesses exceptional organizational leadership skills. He has mentored fellow engineers, supervised projects, and overseen technical aspects with finesse. His capability in implementing new technologies and fostering innovation makes him a dynamic figure in the entrepreneurial landscape.

Anish's contributions extend across borders, as he has successfully helped businesses launch products in various corners of the globe, including the USA, UK, Australia, Canada, and Singapore. His experience in navigating international markets adds a unique global perspective to his insights.

Anish's expertise in overcoming technical hurdles, marketing and branding, and gleaning insights from successful startup founders provides an inspiring roadmap for readers. With a focus on practical approaches and real-life examples, "The Startup Codebook" offers aspiring developer-founders the essential tools and knowledge to navigate the entrepreneurial journey with confidence. Whether you're an experienced developer looking to make the leap into entrepreneurship or a budding entrepreneur seeking to understand the technical landscape, Anish's book is a must-read for those seeking to unlock the code to startup success.